Sparta

Fall of a Warrior Nation

Philip Matyszak

Pen & Sword
MILITARY

First published in Great Britain in 2018 by
PEN & SWORD MILITARY
an imprint of
Pen & Sword Books Ltd
47 Church Street
Barnsley
South Yorkshire
S70 2AS

ISBN 978-1-47387-472-5

Typeset by Concept, Huddersfield HD4 5JL.
Printed and bound in England by TJ International Ltd, Padstow, Cornwall.

Pen & Sword Books Limited incorporates the imprints of Atlas, Archaeology,
Aviation, Discovery, Family History, Fiction, History, Maritime, Military,
Military Classics, Politics, Select, Transport, True Crime, Air World,
Frontline Publishing, Leo Cooper, Remember When, Seaforth Publishing,
The Praetorian Press, Wharncliffe Local History, Wharncliffe Transport,
Wharncliffe True Crime and White Owl.

For a complete list of Pen & Sword titles please contact
PEN & SWORD BOOKS LIMITED
47 Church Street, Barnsley, South Yorkshire, S70 2AS, England
E-mail: enquiries@pen-and-sword.co.uk
Website: www.pen-and-sword.co.uk

Contents

List of Plates

A Spartan points out a drunken slave to his sons; painting by Fernand Sabatte, 1900.

A Persian combat engineer mounted on a donkey.

The entrance to the Temple of Apollo at Delphi.

A Persian archer, from an Athenian black-figure vase.

Greek infantry depicted on a frieze.

The Leonidian in modern Sparta.

The view across Sparta to Mt Parnon.

A contemporary woman's jewellery.

A mother arms her son before battle.

Mount Ithome depicted in an 1882 woodcut.

The medieval monastery at Mystras.

King Nabis, portrait taken from a contemporary coin.

Philip II of Macedon.

The Spartan acropolis looking west across modern Sparta.

Modern Sparta with the Taygetos range in the background.

The remains of the theatre, as seen from the Spartan acropolis.

The remains of the walls of Sparta.

A single olive tree of tough wood, illustrating the difficulty of destroying even a few acres of such trees.

Glossary

agoge	the Spartan system of raising and educating children.
Gerousia	the council of Elders, roughly analogous with a senate.
harmost	a military governor of a town or area.
helots	those bound by the Spartans in a condition between serfdom and slavery.
homoi	the 'Equals' – full Spartan citizens.
kleros	land held by a Spartiate to pay for his upkeep.
krypteia	Spartan spies and assassins.
mothaces	non-Spartiates brought up under the *agoge* system.
navarchos	naval commander.
perioiki	non-Spartans living in Laconia and subject to Sparta although nominally independent.
polemarch	army or phalanx commander.
rhetra	a proposal put to the assembly of the Spartan people.
sarissa	a long pike adopted by Philip II of Macedon.
Spartiates	the top rank of Spartan society.
stasis	civil strife up to and including civil war.
strategos	a general.
syssitia	the Spartan military mess. Non-payment of mess fees reduced a Spartiate from that rank.
tresantes	'Tremblers' – survivors of a losing battle. Again, this title cost a Spartiate his rank.

Introduction

This book is a history of the fall of Sparta. In the chapters to come, we follow Sparta over the course of three centuries as the state descended from being a great power, admired, respected and feared, to a petty state in the Peloponnese, vulnerable to predatory neighbours and almost universally scorned and disliked. In Greek, the word *historia* means 'inquiry' and that inquiry is at the heart of this book. What happened to Sparta? How did the state fall so low? Was it preventable, and what lessons can we learn from that fall?

This inquiry starts in the aftermath of the battle of Plataea in 479 BC. At this time Sparta was the undisputed leader of Greece. How this leadership was lost, and along with it Sparta's moral authority, is one of the themes we shall address. We shall also see how the relentless focus of Sparta's leaders on what was good for Sparta, and for Sparta alone, was both short-sighted and in the long run actually very bad for Sparta.

The Peloponnesian War should have allowed Sparta to secure the dominance of Greece in the same way that the Pyrrhic War established Rome's control of Italy. Yet Rome went on to found an empire, while Sparta proceeded towards a shambolic collapse. Much of the content of this book involves the Peloponnesian War and its aftermath. This is because it is important to show why, although Sparta seemed to emerge from the conflict triumphant, this was a very different victory from that which Sparta had won over the Persians in the previous century. Sparta emerged from fighting off the Persian invaders as a self-confident society, and a beacon for the Greeks of the day. After the Peloponnesian War Sparta's moral authority was in tatters, its society fractured, and its political capital squandered. Sparta won that war, but at the same time it lost Greece.

As we follow Sparta's attempts to maintain the hegemony of Greece after the Peloponnesian War, the intellectual sterility of the state is revealed as never before. Athens was far from admirable in very many ways, but no one in Greece denied that Athens had much to offer. In the arts, in science and in philosophy, the Athenians were pushing the human race forward with a boundless (and often disturbing) intellectual freedom and ambition. At first Sparta seemed also to stand for something – the nobility of sacrifice, the power of discipline and the use of these attributes to fight for the freedom of tiny Greece against a huge and expansionist empire.

Yet in exchange for domination in Greece, the Spartans traded away exactly those qualities for which their city was admired – and traded them to the Persians in exchange for political support and a lot of money. Thereafter Sparta offered only a mindless conservatism combined with an amoral militarism which had no higher purpose than maintaining Sparta's hold on power.

Unsurprisingly, the rest of Greece rejected this vision (if 'vision' is the right word here), and rejected it vehemently. When Thebes rose to ascendancy, what Thebes stood for was that It Was Not Sparta. By then Sparta was so disliked that much of Greece fell in behind Thebes on that count alone. Tellingly, when Thebans in the third century were said to be 'acting like the Spartans', this was intended and received as a dire accusation. Two centuries before it would have been a high compliment.

At a time when the Romans were expanding their civic body (sometimes by the wholesale incorporation of entire communities, however unwilling), the Spartans completely refused to share their citizenship or their power – not with their allies, not with the other people of Laconia, and not even with their own 'inferior' citizens. There were very many ways by which a Spartiate could drop from his rank, and other than by birth almost none by which that rank could be attained. As we shall see, this meant that over the centuries the privileges of Spartiate rank belonged to a small and ever-shrinking circle. A constant theme in this book is the ever-diminishing number of Spartiates, and their reluctance to expand this group or share its benefits, even though this exclusionism was very much against the welfare of the state which the Spartiates claimed to embody.

In short, this book is a study of a downward social spiral and an object lesson in the dangers of short-sighted chauvinism in inter-state relationships. The fall of Sparta was not inevitable – and the lessons of how that fall could have been prevented are not applicable to Sparta alone. For the admirers of Sparta – and they are many – the tragedy of this tale is not that Sparta fell. The tragedy is what Sparta became before it fell.

Chapter 1

The State of the Nation – Sparta in 478 BC

The battles of Plataea and Mycale in the year 479 BC had brought the Persian Wars if not to an end, at least to a standstill. Now that hostilities had ceased, Sparta found itself at a crossroads. When Persia threatened Greece, all the Greeks had turned to Sparta for leadership, and Sparta had delivered. True, this had been leadership rather than generalship, because Sparta's commanders had acquitted themselves poorly in terms of tactical ability. However, the fighting skill of Sparta's hoplites had on each occasion saved their city's reputation. Consequently Sparta emerged from the Persian Wars admired and respected by the rest of Greece.

The question was, what did Sparta intend to do with this new reserve of political capital? If the Spartans wanted it, continued leadership of the Hellenic League was theirs for the asking. This in turn would have meant expanding Spartan horizons beyond the Peloponnese to the coast of Asia Minor, and increasing the Spartan hegemony from the Peloponnesian League to the city-states of the Aegean Sea. It was a challenging role, and no doubt many Spartans would have been happy to assume it.

Certainly among these was Pausanias, the Spartan general who had commanded with a fair degree of incompetence at Plataea, and who was now enjoying his role as a Spartan potentate representing Sparta's interests abroad. However, like many Spartans who ventured outside the repressive bounds of their own society, Pausanias proved unable to cope. Greek cities with which he had dealings found him to be arrogant and high-handed, and a growing flow of complaints about his conduct began to reach the Ephors in Sparta.

Perhaps this 'ingratitude' from liberated Greek states was what caused the Spartans to withdraw from active involvement with the Hellenic League. Other historians, and also contemporary Greeks, saw this as an example of Spartan conservatism and timidity – a failure to boldly grasp the opportunity of consolidating the city's position as the foremost state of Greece. With the Spartans apparently uninterested in the challenges of leadership, control of the League fell to the highly enterprising, ambitious and amoral Athenians, a people whose appetite for a challenge was never in doubt.

So why, once the Persian Wars had ended, did Sparta step back from the leadership of Greece? Was it indeed innate Spartan conservatism married to a fear of new developments? Certainly Sparta was always insular and parochial. The city's position in the southern Peloponnese meant it could hardly be otherwise. Congenial as was the city's actual location on the banks of the Eurotas river, Sparta was never going to become an international metropolis, because it was also not the most accessible of cities.

Approach from the sea was hazardous even in those months when the season was good for sailing. The only route was from the south, where the twin capes of Malea and Taenaron had a fearsome reputation for wrecking ships. Between them, these promontories virtually closed off the sea approaches to Laconia from the east and west. Further north, on land, approaches from east and west were equally difficult. On either side of the Eurotas valley were mountain ranges with passes varying from precipitous to downright inaccessible. Given these challenges to access, for much of the year the only approach to Sparta was through a series of convoluted mountain passes to the north. Thus Sparta was a city designed by nature to be a quiet backwater, set aside from the hectic strife of Greek politics. While the whole world could, and did, send visitors and goods streaming through the ports of Athens and Corinth, visitors to Sparta were rare (and not particularly welcome) and trade goods were scarce.

Yet despite the natural disadvantages of the city's location, Sparta had over the preceding centuries risen to become the foremost nation of Greece. This rise, and almost every other significant aspect of Spartan life, had one basic cause – Messenia. The effect of Messenia on Sparta (and the effect of Sparta on Messenia) is hard to overstate. Throughout the history of classical Greece these two states were locked together in a grim and dysfunctional relationship which for the Spartans was both a blessing and a curse, and for the Messenians was an unmitigated curse.

It was the conquest of Messenia in the eighth century BC that had changed Sparta from a somewhat standard second-rank Greek city into one of the leading states of Greece. The agricultural wealth of Messenia became the wealth of Sparta. Because the subject population of Messenia worked that land on behalf of Spartan masters, Sparta itself could afford to support what at that time was the only professional warrior caste in Greece. Because full citizen males (called 'Spartiates') did nothing but train for war, they were very good at waging it. For most of the century preceding the Persian Wars it was a given that any state that met the Spartans in battle was going to lose, and this perception made up a great proportion of the vast respect that the Spartans were afforded.

However, there was also a dark side to the conquest of Messenia. If conquering the place had made Sparta the leading state in Greece, holding on to that conquest took almost everything Sparta had to give. Control of Messenia was neither cheap nor easy. Partly this was because the Messenians and Spartans were much alike: proud, unforgiving and un-yielding. Certainly this was why the original conquest of Messenia had taken so long and had involved Sparta in employing dirty tricks and faithless diplomacy as much as military valour.

Yet the main difficulty for Sparta lay in the major difference between Spartans and Messenians – the latter were much more numerous, and their land was both larger and more prosperous. It is sometimes forgotten that mighty Sparta was in fact a confederation of four villages. At a rough estimate, the area of 'metropolitan' Sparta was some 50 square miles, with a population of some 30,000 citizens. At full stretch, fifth-century Sparta could put 5,000 hoplites in the field – although this number was con-siderably augmented by the contributions of other Laconian towns of *perioiki* and members of the Peloponnesian League.

By contrast Messenia, at some 11,000 square miles in area, was well over 200 times larger than Sparta, though the figure is exaggerated by large areas of uninhabitable mountain range and wilderness. Nevertheless, even if we assume just 20 per cent of Messenia was occupied, this still gives an area easily ten times larger than Sparta. This is reflected in population numbers. Despite the absence of anything vaguely resembling a Spartan statistic, some estimates can be made from archaeological research and from figures such as the number of helots brought by the Spartans to the battle of Plataea (35,000 according to Herodotus).

These data, combined with a study of the population numbers in nineteenth-century Messenia (when agricultural development was about the same), have led historians to extrapolate a population of some 130,000–175,000 Messenians. How many of these Messenians would have formed an army of liberation is impossible to tell, because of the dedicated and ruthless efforts of the Spartans to prevent such an army from forming.

However, it is revealing that the Spartans operated on the rule of thumb that every Spartiate had to be the military equivalent of seven to ten Messenians. This does not necessarily give us a potential Messenian army of 50,000, because the Spartans were realistic enough to acknowledge that if they had to cope with a full-scale Messenian war, they would probably have to deal with a few other opportunistic enemies as well. Nevertheless, we can assume that Messenia was probably capable of putting 25,000 poorly armed but highly enthusiastic warriors into the field at very short notice. In other words, even if facing no other enemies and with no other commitments abroad, the Spartan army started off by being outnumbered five to one.

In short, in their occupation of Messenia, the Spartans had a tiger by the tail, and they were well aware of this. As Aristotle remarked of the helots and a similar subject population in Thessaly:

> For the Penestae in Thessaly made frequent attacks on the Thessalians, as did the Helots upon the Lacedaemonians; indeed, they may be described as perpetually lying in wait to take advantage of their masters' misfortunes. (Aristotle, *Politics*, 2.9)

Having occupied Messenia, the Spartans had no choice but to continue with that occupation. The Messenians had generations of pent-up ill-will against Sparta, and if the Spartans were for some reason to abandon their conquest and leave the Messenians to their own devices, few Spartans doubted what would be the first act of a free Messenia: it would be to make sure that Sparta could never come back – preferably because Sparta had been pounded into a smoking pile of rubble. In short, the occupation of Messenia had to continue because this was seen as a precondition for the continued existence of Sparta.

The Spartan technique for controlling Messenia was basically rule by terror. Any Messenian who showed signs of leadership or enterprise, in no matter how harmless a direction, was promptly assassinated by the *krypteia*, an organization of Spartan youths dedicated to this purpose. To legitimize these acts of murder, the Spartan authorities ritually opened hostilities with the helots at the start of every year, so the killings became an act of war. Despite this, there were times when more extreme measures were considered necessary, and as will be seen, nor did the Spartans flinch from these.

Given that the Spartan occupation of Messenia consisted of centuries of unsympathetic oppression, and that the Spartans were universally hated by their victims, it is to this, rather than to any innate Spartan conservatism or timidity, that we should attribute Sparta's lack of interest in foreign adventure. The reason why every male Spartan was a warrior, the reason why the state was ruthlessly optimized for war, was because Sparta had to strain every sinew to keep Messenia in check.

Sparta had just 5,000 warriors. History has shown that this number was enough to keep Messenia down. But it did not leave much manpower available for anything else. The idea that the Spartan army could be gone for months at a time on campaign in Asia Minor was a fantasy. States like Athens could, and sometimes did, send almost every able-bodied male off on a foreign adventure, secure in the knowledge that the people at home were solidly behind them. The Spartan army had not that luxury. The moment the helots figured out that their oppressors were not coming back any time soon, they would not only throw off their chains, but also descend on Sparta itself with the intent of bloodily wiping out three centuries of grudges.

This was the basic fact behind all Spartan foreign policy, and a fact that the Spartans tried very hard to hide from their neighbours. Every act of Spartan policy had to be weighed against the consideration 'How will this affect our control of Messenia?', and if the answer meant avoiding embroilment abroad, and keeping the Spartan army as close to home as possible, this was only to be expected. If Sparta was conservative, it was because the Spartans had much to lose from any change to the status quo. If the Spartans sometimes appeared timid, it was because they had much to fear.

The companion volume to this book (Philip Matyszak, *Sparta, Rise of a Warrior Nation*, Pen & Sword, 2017) has shown that, as Sparta expanded its power towards the northern Peloponnese, it quickly became apparent that a Messenian-like subjugation of the northern neighbours was not practicable. Simply put, it was all Sparta could do to hold down the subject population it already had, without adding to that number. Nevertheless, places like Tegea and Arcadia had to be brought within the Spartan hegemony out of simple self-preservation. In the past both areas had taken an unhealthy interest in dragging Messenia into their political struggles. If those struggles were against Sparta, then stirring up trouble in Messenia was a guaranteed distraction, and in other situations there was no doubt that whatever state prised Messenia out of Sparta's clutches would ever-more have a powerful and deeply grateful ally.

This, it has been argued, was the main intent behind the Peloponnesian League. The League was less an instrument which Sparta intended to use against enemies further afield than the means by which Sparta prevented enemies close to home from uniting against Sparta itself. After all, the best way to prevent a state from allying against Sparta was to have that state already allied to Sparta – and sworn to help Sparta against anyone else who demonstrated anti-Spartan proclivities. That this was the intention in forming the League is clear from the nature of the treaties between Sparta and League members. Individual member states had no obligation or treaty agreements with any other League state – their alliance was with Sparta alone.

Because the Peloponnesian League was basically formed to protect Sparta from those states which made up its membership, Sparta had little interest in expanding the League. There was no reason to include – for example – cities of the Anatolian seaboard. In Spartan minds, the danger to Sparta from other states was directly proportional to their proximity to Messenia. Cities on the other side of the Aegean Sea were too far away to pose any such threat, and consequently there was no point in binding them into the League.

If, as is sometimes assumed, the Peloponnesian League had indeed been an instrument of Spartan imperialism, then certainly adding cities from further abroad would have increased the League's power and reach – but increased power and reach were not the purpose of the League. It was not about expanding Sparta's possessions but about helping Sparta to hold on to what it already had.

There was, of course, one Peloponnesian state which was not a member of the League, and that was Argos. This ancient and powerful city might be assumed to have been a massive threat to Sparta, yet in the generation before the Persian Wars the Spartans had spurned an opportunity to destroy Argos altogether. Why?

Upon reflection, it can be argued that the existence of Argos was sufficiently beneficial for it to be in Sparta's interest that Argos remained powerful – up to a point. For a start, in Argos, as in every other contemporary Greek state, warfare was practically a seasonal hobby for the hoplite class. Historically, the Argives had a habit of fighting these wars against their somewhat smaller and weaker Peloponnesian neighbours. Therefore, the Spartans could point out to League members that it was only their alliance with Sparta that kept Argos off their backs. Defection from the League might or might not mean war with Sparta, but sooner or later it would certainly mean war with Argos.

This argument worked both with the League's lesser members and with the largest and most awkward of the Spartan allies, the city of Corinth. To some extent Peloponnesian politics consisted of the wary interaction between three powerful city-states: Sparta, Argos and Corinth. Wealthy, worldly, cosmopolitan and slightly decadent, Corinth had absolutely nothing in common with Sparta apart from the one thing which kept this unlikely pair as allies – a desire to keep Argos firmly under control.

Therefore, from the Spartan point of view, having Argos around meant that two powerful cities – Sparta and Corinth – combined forces to control a third – Argos. Removing Argos from the equation would actually be disadvantageous, as it would also remove the only thing keeping Sparta and Corinth allied. Without Argos, instead of two powerful cities facing down a third, this would leave Sparta and Corinth – near equals in power – facing off against each other: a serious deterioration of the odds.

In other words, Sparta needed the Peloponnesian League, and to keep both large and small members within the League, Sparta needed Argos. Preferably Argos should be hostile but relatively impotent. Probably not coincidentally that condition broadly describes Argos both in the generation before the Persian Wars and for the generation thereafter.

Thus when we look at the position of Sparta immediately after the Persian Wars, we can see that the state's leaders had good reason to be satisfied. If we consider that the prime Spartan objective in foreign policy was to ensure that nothing threatened the Spartan grip on Messenia, then things were looking good. Those close to Sparta were allies or subjects, and those further away regarded Sparta with anything from wary respect to outright admiration.

Spartan leadership had been essential in rallying the Greeks against the Persian invader, partly because of the respect in which Sparta was already held. However, Greek unity in the face of the Persians also came about partly because the Spartans made it clear that, should the invasion be successfully repulsed, there would be a reckoning with anyone who had broken ranks. Of all the Greek states, Sparta was best equipped to deliver on that threat.

Now that Greece was safe and the Persian invasion had been repulsed, there can be little doubt that both Sparta and Persia would have happily negotiated peace if there was some way to do so and save face. From the Persian point of view, a defeat of the magnitude that they had just suffered had repercussions all around their empire. The sprawling multitude of states that made up Persia's dominions had little in common other than a healthy respect for the Persian army. As news of the defeat of that army rippled through the empire, it was inevitable that the thoughts of independent-minded nations would turn to rebellion. This was especially true of the Egyptians, conscious of their thousands of years of history as an independent state, and bitterly resentful of Persian rule. It is probably in this context of internal unrest that the Persian king Xerxes executed the governor of independent-minded Bactra, rather than the lurid tale of inter-harem feuding described by Herodotus (Book 9, 110ff).

Overall the Persians would rather have liked to pretend that the Greek adventure had never happened, and would prefer to simply wash their hands of those recalcitrant and annoyingly well armed peoples to the west. They could then get on with calming the restive nations already under their control before they focused on expansion in a more profitable direction. The problem for Persia was one of public perception, since making peace at this point could not be seen as anything but a clear admission of defeat, and the Persians were not prepared to take this step just yet. For propaganda reasons the Persians had to pretend that, while their plans had suffered a setback, Operation Conquer Greece was still a going concern and the invincible Persian war machine was simply manoeuvring to find a fresh way around the current obstacles. So Persia remained at war with the Greeks, while being careful to do as little actual fighting as possible.

From the Spartan perspective, the Persian Wars had been fought to keep the Persians out of Greece. Now that objective had been achieved, Sparta had little reason to keep fighting. Hitherto Sparta had shown little affection for or interest in the cities of Ionia, regarding them mainly as a fortunate distraction which kept the Athenians from meddling in the affairs of central Greece. Now, with Sparta pushed into leadership of the Hellenic League, the cities of Ionia looked to the Spartans to supply that leadership, and the nonplussed Spartans were somewhat at a loss about how to supply it.

A peace with Persia that left the Ionian cities to their own devices would have been ideal. However, the Ionians saw a chance to harm the Persian giant while it was wounded. They wanted to continue the war, with or without Sparta. Nor were the Spartans themselves united on the issue. Some welcomed the opportunity to consolidate their city's hegemony over the entire Greek people. Others, looking nervously over their shoulders at the Messenian mountains, passionately disagreed.

Thus it is a mistake to assume that after success against the Persians, peace on the domestic front continued within Sparta itself. Certainly, the Lycurgan system had proven its worth. The 300 had died uncomplainingly – even proudly – at Thermopylae, and though inept Spartan generalship had left them exposed against an enemy five times their number, the Spartan hoplites at Plataea had unflinchingly held firm and eventually triumphed. Surely, therefore, all Sparta had to do for continued success was to maintain the system which had produced warriors such as these? Everyone in Greece knew the Spartan character – laconic but shrewd, honourable to a fault, indifferent to pain and luxury alike, and always disciplined and fearless.

Of course, one of the reasons why everyone knew what the Spartans were like is because the Spartans were so insular that not many Greeks actually met Spartans face-to-face in a social setting. An unexpected problem arising from Sparta's leadership of the Hellenic League was that it regularly brought other Greeks into close contact with those Spartans at the helm. All too often reality brought disillusion. The Spartan mystique proved distressingly vulnerable to the very human foibles of actual Spartans.

Therefore it should come as no surprise that, far from being quietly satisfied with the success Sparta had achieved through the strengths of its unique society, the Spartan leadership was instead riven by a fierce debate about how best to exploit that success. One of the major advantages of the Spartan constitution was that power was divided between aristocrats, kings and Ephors. Socially too, Spartan citizens were encouraged to think of themselves as *homoi* – equals. The disadvantage of this system was that at a time when clear leadership and direction were required, different factions of the Spartan leadership had very clear but mutually incompatible ideas of what direction Sparta should take. From peace, quiet satisfaction and harmony at home, Sparta's success thereafter divided the nation to the extent that the state was incapable of formulating any coherent foreign policy at all.

Consequently Sparta's allies were left to watch the frustrating spectacle of Sparta simultaneously pursuing several incompatible objectives, but pursuing none with any purpose or conviction. To the outsider's eye, this looked a lot like indecisive dithering, and it was far from the image Sparta wanted or needed to present. At the very moment of Sparta's greatest triumph the first cracks in the system were becoming alarmingly evident.

Chapter 2

The First Cracks

Not unexpectedly, one of the keenest proponents of the policy that Sparta should remain leader of the Hellenic League and that Spartan power should be projected as far abroad as possible was the man currently doing the leading and projecting. This was Pausanias, the Spartan commander of the Hellenic League. It is often suggested that one reason why Pausanias was determined to keep Sparta – and therefore himself – at the forefront of Greek affairs was because he himself was not the leader of Sparta, and therefore stepping down from his role with the Hellenic League would have entailed a major demotion.

Not only was Pausanias not the leader of Sparta, he was also not a king. He was merely a regent standing in until Pleistarchus, the actual king, reached maturity. When the now-revered king Leonidas had fallen at Thermopylae in 480, his son had inherited his office while being too young to exercise its functions. Originally that task had belonged to a brother of Leonidas, but Pausanias, as a member of the Agaid family, had inherited the regency on the brother's death and now performed regal duties on his cousin's behalf. However, once Pleistarchus reached his majority Pausanias would have some influence but little power.

Admittedly, the Spartan kingship had long ago ceased to be an autocracy within Sparta, having been kneecapped by the institution of the Ephorate since at least 700 BC. ('Because the power of the Ephors is excessive and dictatorial, even the Spartan kings are forced to grovel to them,' remarks Aristotle cheerfully [*Politics*, 2.9], adding that because they were not themselves always wealthy, the Ephors had a very un-Spartan weakness for bribes.) Still, the kingship was a position which an ambitious man could use to obtain a position of power.

King Leotychides and 'northern dominance'
Of course, as well as a regent and a stripling lad, Sparta also had an actual, mature reigning king. Sparta's constitution was averse to autocracy, so it ensured that the highest office of state, the kingship, was not only checked by the Ephorate but also shared between two royal families. Pausanias (via Pleistarchus) ruled for the Agaid family. His opposite number for the

royal Eurypontid line was Leotychides, a monarch who had enjoyed success during the Persian Wars. He was commander of the forces which had destroyed the Persian fleet at Mycale in 479 – a feat achieved on the very day that Pausanias defeated the land army at Plataea in mainland Greece.

Despite this shared history of victory over the Persians, it appears that Sparta's leaders had incompatible visions of Sparta's role in the future. While Pausanias looked eastward to engaging with Persia and the Greek cities of Asia Minor, Leotychides was intent on securing Sparta's leadership on the Greek mainland, and on reducing the rest of Greece to the status of subject allies, as the nations of the Peloponnese were already.

These two projects – Pausanias projecting Greek power abroad while Leotychides was simultaneously seeking mastery of the very Greeks doing that projecting – were exceptionally difficult, but not impossible, to combine into one coherent policy. The Athenians were to have a good crack at achieving that very feat a decade later. However, the Athenians were helped by the masterly political skill first of Themistocles and then of Pericles, while foreign policy in Sparta was hindered by the Ephors.

Just as Spartan kings (and regents) exercised their greatest power while operating outside Laconia, the Ephors were most powerful at home. Always mindful of their role of keeping Sparta's kings in check, the Ephors not surprisingly wanted the Spartan kings out of foreign adventures and back in Sparta where they were firmly under the Ephoric thumb. Consequently, while the Agaid and Eurypontid rulers each pursued an independent foreign policy, each blithely uncaring what his royal colleague was up to, the Ephors were at work at home assiduously undermining the efforts of both. Due to the natural human tendency to conflate the general good with self-interest, at least initially all these protagonists probably had the genuine belief that they were working in Sparta's best interests as well as their own. None of the three parties seems to have been aware of how demoralizing this disjointed policy was to Sparta's supporters abroad. If they were aware of the damage they were doing to Sparta's image, this served as an incentive for them to ensure that their particular vision succeeded as soon as possible.

First to suffer a setback was the Leotychides policy of subjugating Greece. We have seen that the two Peloponnesian cities of Argos and Corinth were largely nullified by Sparta playing one off against the other. For the rest of Greece, the major powers were Boeotia (dominated by Thebes), Attica (which was basically Athens), and Thessaly.

For the moment Thebes was out of the game. The city had unwisely sided with the Persians in the recent war. At the climactic battle of Plataea the Theban phalanx had been mauled but not massacred by the Athenians. Thereafter, Thebes was faced by the united enmity of Greece led by the unforgiving Spartans, who besieged the city for twenty days. Thebes was forced to surrender its pro-Persian leaders to Pausanias, and those who did not flee in time were taken to Corinth. There Pausanias had the men arbitrarily executed.

This execution certainly saved time since any form of tribunal would certainly have found the men guilty of betraying the Greek cause. Nevertheless executing the traitors without so much as a hearing caused a degree of unease. In Sparta this unease was directed at the autocratic conduct of Pausanias, but the rest of Greece assumed the arbitrary mindset behind the executions was that of Sparta in general, and this led to suspicion about how Sparta intended to proceed.

As a result of this suspicion, when Sparta argued that any cities which had previously fought on the Persian side should be excluded from the Hellenic League, the proposal met with serious opposition. This opposition was led by Themistocles of the Athenians, who rightly pointed out that Thebes and Argos were the only pro-Persian cities of any significance. If Thebes were sidelined, then the influence of the remaining major powers in Greece – especially Athens and Sparta – would be correspondingly increased. This was, of course, the Spartan intention. Leotychides already had plans in train for controlling Athens, and Argos was already checked by Corinth. Therefore if Thebes were taken out of the diplomatic picture this would leave only Thessaly to be brought under Spartan control.

However, the Spartan motion was defeated, and Thebes, annoyingly, remained a first-rank political power. Defeat of his motion at Athenian hands made Leotychides accelerate his plans to interfere in Athenian affairs. One also suspects that the execution of the Theban leaders by Pausanias had played a part in alienating the other Greeks, and this led Leotychides to believe that, like the Athenians, Pausanias also needed to be speedily brought under control.

At Corinth, Pausanias had consecrated to the Gods the best of the spoils looted from the Persians at Plataea with the following dedication:

> The Hellenic General Pausanias, who defeated the Persians, has consecrated this gift to Phoebus [Apollo] as a record of his deeds.
>
> (Thucydides, *The Peloponnesian War*, 1.132)

But the Ephors and Leotychides were having none of it, and scored a somewhat petty point by scrubbing the name of Pausanias from the inscription and replacing it with a list of the confederate Greek states which had fought in the battle.

This small victory aside, Leotychides needed a major policy success. For the moment he could not stop Thebes and Argos from becoming fully-fledged members of the League, but there remained Thessaly. Like Thebes and Athens, Thessaly was one of those states that had to be brought to heel if Sparta were to dominate Greece as it already dominated the Peloponnese.

It helped greatly that an attack on Thessaly was one of those areas where the personal interests of Leotychides, his ambitions for Sparta, and the general interest of the Greeks were aligned. Like Thebes, Thessaly had taken the Persian side in the invasion by Xerxes. This was not because Thessaly's leading dynasty, the Aleuadae, were particularly pro-Persian in ideology, but because with the rest of Greece already contemplating retreat to the Peloponnese, Thessaly had been left alone and exposed to the full Persian force. The Aleuadae had taken the only sensible course of action and submitted to the oncoming army of at least 100,000 well-armed opponents.

However, given the heroics of Leonidas and the 300 on the Thessalian border, the actions of the Aleuadae could be interpreted not as pragmatic, but as craven or even treasonous. At this early juncture, the Greeks were not sure whether their defeat of the Persians was the resounding victory it seemed or the mere setback that Persian propaganda was claiming. Therefore, argued Leotychides, if the Persians were indeed to come again, it would be best if the Aleuadae were not in Thessaly to once again open the door to the invaders. Fortunately (as always in any Greek state) there was a party of malcontents opposed to the current regime, and by a happy coincidence these malcontents were pro-Spartan aristocrats. All seemed to be shaping up for a neat coup which would further the policy of Leotychides. Thanks in part to the conduct of Pausanias, Leotychides had lost face on the diplomatic front. However, dealing with Thessaly would be accomplished not with diplomacy but with military force. This, Leotychides might have assured himself, was one area in which Sparta could not fail. Thessaly would become a Spartan puppet and, with Spartan-dominated states to the north and south, further pressure could be brought on Athens and Thebes.

The troops with which Leotychides intended to subjugate Thrace were drawn from the Hellenic League forces near Byzantium. The other Greeks objected strenuously to this division of the army, especially the loss of Spartan hoplites. This probably counted as a bonus for

Leotychides, who was thus able to score a few more points against Pausanias, who lost face with the other Greeks because he was clearly unable to prevent the Spartans from hiving off troops from his army.

The Walls of Athens

At the same time as his expedition set off for Thessaly, Leotychides launched his planned policy initiative against Athens. Sparta, as delegates to Athens disingenuously pointed out, famously had no city walls. Nor did any other settlement in Laconia. The peace of the unwalled region was in stark contrast to the strife-torn remainder of Greece. Why not, urged the delegates, leave the rest of Greece as unwalled as Laconia? Just as in Laconia, Spartan arms would be enough to defend the cities against outside threat, and without the assurance of city walls to protect them, states would be much less likely to go to war between themselves. Furthermore, walls had not prevented the Persians from mastering Thebes, but the Theban city walls had given the Persians a strong base in central Greece once Thebes had been mastered.

Therefore, it was argued, it was best that no city north of Corinth had walls. Nor did the Athenians have to throw down their city walls: the Persian invaders had already done the job for them. All Athens had to do to comply with this Spartan initiative was to leave the city's walls unreconstructed. As a state that claimed to be one of the leaders of Greece, here was a chance for Athens painlessly to demonstrate leadership by doing absolutely nothing.

By way of demonstrating Spartan sincerity, Leotychides might have pointed out publicly that the men were already allocated for the defence of Athens should the need arise. Privately, the Athenians could be made aware that these same men could also be deployed *against* Athens – which was currently almost defenceless – in the event of Athens engaging in any activities hostile to Sparta. Rebuilding the walls would count as one of those hostile acts.

As the Peloponnesian Wars of the next generation were to demonstrate, if Athens did not have walls – and strong walls – there was nothing to stop Sparta's army from walking on to the Athenian agora any time it fancied, and there laying down Spartan terms for the ruling of the state. Therefore, if the Athenians were to comply with this diplomatically disguised order, at a stroke Spartan dominance of Attica would have been established. Consequently, the Spartan proposal was greeted with consternation and dismay in Athens.

In this moment of crisis the man to whom all turned was that same wily Themistocles who had plotted the course of Athenian strategy at Salamis – and indeed from much earlier. According to his biographer Plutarch, it was Themistocles who had earlier persuaded the Athenians to make the investment in the Athenian fleet which had made the victory at Salamis possible (Plutarch, *Themistocles*, 4).

The historian Thucydides takes up the tale:

> Thus the Lacedaemonians made their presentation. Immediately afterwards, on the advice of Themistocles, they were promptly dismissed from the city. The Spartans took with them the [Athenian] answer that ambassadors would be sent to Sparta to discuss the entire issue. Themistocles told the Athenians to make him the first of these ambassadors, and he would go to Sparta immediately. However, the Athenians were to take as much time as possible choosing his ambassadorial colleagues ...
>
> When he arrived at Sparta, Themistocles did not try to arrange any meetings with the government, but gained extra time with excuses. When the authorities questioned why he did not appear in the Assembly [to present Athenian views], he replied that he was awaiting the other ambassadors. In fact he professed amazement that they had not already arrived, saying that they must be engaged with something important.

In reality, back in Athens every available man was working on rebuilding the wall, with his wife and children working alongside him. It was a desperate high-speed effort that not only recycled those parts of the wall which the Persians had left strewn across the landscape, but also sacrificed to the cause any likely collection of masonry – even if that masonry currently made up a public building or private house.

Here the relative isolation of Sparta acted against the city's best interest, because travellers from Athens were few (and doubtless even those few found their travel plans to Sparta strenuously discouraged by the Athenians). Therefore news of the Athenian wall-building project reached Sparta much more slowly than the walls themselves were rising.

> At first the Spartans trusted Themistocles, because he had previously been on friendly terms with them. Yet travellers kept arriving, and each claimed that there were not only walls going up, but that these walls were rather high already. After a while these reports became all too credible. However, Themistocles argued that these travellers were merely repeating untrustworthy rumours as if they were real news.

If the Spartans really wanted to know what was going on, they should send a trusted observer who would report back – after a proper inspection – on how things stood.

However, Themistocles sent ahead a messenger to warn [the Athenians] that this observer should be [politely] detained and not allowed to go until Themistocles and his fellow ambassadors had returned to Athens.

In this way the Athenians walled their city in record time. Even now the walls show signs of the speed with which they were built. The foundations consist of stones of different kinds, not carved or organized but simply laid down as soon as whoever arrived with fresh supplies. Many columns are built into the walls as well, along with material from tombs, and sculptures jammed in with the rest.

(Thucydides, *The Peloponnesian War*, 1.4, *passim*)

Thus it came about that when Themistocles finally had to face the Spartan assembly, he bluntly told them that Athens had decided to refute their suggestion of Spartan 'protection' and rebuild the city walls instead. In fact, the Athenians already had these walls, and any future Spartan suggestions about Athenian defence should be made on the assumption that the Athenians were quite capable of looking after their own best interests.

According to Thucydides, the Spartans showed no anger at this speech. Instead they merely commented mildly that their suggestion had been intended as being in the best interests of Greece as a whole. Indeed, they took it so well that Plutarch, in his biography of Themistocles, suggests that the Ephors and other leading men had been forewarned of this development and bribed by Themistocles to go along with it.

However, if we accept that the proposal to denude northern Greek cities of their walls was part of the strategy by which Leotychides intended to enforce the Spartan dominance of Greece, we must perforce also accept that the Ephors did not really need bribing. From the point of view of the Ephors, the sooner Athens had its own walls, the sooner Sparta need not be concerned with the city. All they had to do was turn a wilfully blind eye to the Athenian rebuilding programme and any responsibility Sparta had for the defence of Athens was gone.

Then, like the proposed and failed exclusion of Argos and Thebes from the League, yet another of Leotychides' diplomatic efforts to keep Sparta engaged beyond the Peloponnese would have failed ignominiously. Sparta would be one step further back towards the *status quo ante bellum* – that happy state of affairs before the Persian menace had first appeared, when

Sparta dominated the Peloponnese, and was quite happy to let the rest of the world go hang.

Leotychides in Thessaly

While Themistocles was prevaricating in Sparta with his wall-building skulduggery, Leotychides was having a less than happy time in Thessaly. His experience revealed another reason why perhaps the Ephors were wise to insist that the Spartans should keep their activities south of the isthmus of Corinth. The Spartan army was undoubtedly a superb war machine, but it was a war machine that had evolved exclusively for operations within the highly specialized conditions of the Peloponnese.

Within the Peloponnese the flat land required for hoplite warfare was at a premium – indeed to the extent where hoplites sometimes had to wait in line for their chance to enter a highly congested battlefield. On such occasions, the Spartans only had to worry about defeating the enemy directly in front of them – something they could do with magnificent aplomb. Matters like flanking forces were largely made irrelevant due to lack of space in which to do any flanking, and cavalry forces were literally an afterthought unleashed to make a fleeing enemy even more miserable. Furthermore, the Spartans were accustomed to operating in an environment where a friendly, or at worst cowed, civilian populace offered little resistance to the passage of the army.

None of this applied in Thessaly. Thessaly was, and is, a land of wide-open plains deeply cut by river valleys. The dominant Aleuadae clan might not have been particularly democratic, but the local peasantry quite rightly calculated that any rivals to the Aleuadae who were supported by the autocratic Spartans were even less likely to be on their side. Therefore public sentiment supported the Aleuadae against the invaders. Furthermore, power in Thessaly was more devolved than in most areas of Greece. This meant that almost every local leader had a fair degree of autonomy, and most used this to resist the Spartan presence with varying degrees of vehemence.

In the wide open plains the Spartans found that the Thessalian cavalry could literally ride rings around them. This meant that not only did considerable effort have to be made to protect the front and rear of the Spartan phalanx, but also that there was no way of securing the army's supply lines, since the Thessalian cavalry was free to raid these lines at any point. Therefore the Spartan army needed to live off the land to an even greater extent than was usual for a hoplite army. This certainly did not endear Leotychides to the local peasantry who were already living off that same land and were highly unappreciative of Spartan depredations.

Where the terrain was disrupted by rivers which flow across Thessaly eastwards to the sea, the Spartan phalanx was incapable of maintaining formation and was vulnerable to the hit-and-run tactics of Thessaly's lightly armed but highly mobile citizen soldiery. Because Thessaly spent much of its time in political ferment, these soldiers had plenty of practice at warfare arising from civil strife.

This civil strife also meant that the cities were comprehensively equipped with the same sort of walls that had distressed Leotychides in Athens and other Greek cities further south. At this point in the military development of Greece, siege warfare was in its infancy. If the defenders retreated behind city walls, all that an opposing army could do was sit outside and wait for them to come out. Given time, lack of food would eventually force the defenders to come to terms.

However, Thessalian cities were no strangers to sieges, and most had taken care to equip themselves with abundant food reserves. This contrasted with the Spartan situation, because with Thessalian cavalry causing havoc to their food chain the Spartans had to keep moving or swiftly exhaust the amount of food that could be obtained locally.

Therefore it is not hard to imagine a campaign in which Leotychides met with little resistance in the field. His enemies refused to meet him in open battle, and simply skirmished around the edges of his army. When the Spartans approached a Thessalian city, that city simply closed its gates and waited until the Spartans were forced to go away again in search of their next meal. In terms of suasion, Leotychides achieved the opposite of his intentions. A region that had been mixed in loyalties to the Aleuadae and the Hellenic cause became, after every encounter with the Spartans, less pro-Greek and more pro-Aleuadae.

The contemporary historian Herodotus felt that Leotychides had the region at his mercy, and indeed it is true that the Thessalians could not stand against him. However, they did not have to. They simply had to get out of the way and wait for Leotychides and his army to move on, and that is what they did. Therefore it is very probable that Leotychides was already contemplating abandoning the campaign as an unproductive waste of time when the Aleuadae offered further incentives in the form of a very substantial bribe. Few people are disinclined to accept payment for something they are going to do anyway, so even to a morally upright Spartan there would seem to have been few reasons not to accept the Aleuadae money.

Of course, this is assuming that Leotychides was a morally upright Spartan. Many of his contemporaries who showed a thoroughly Spartan contempt for money and soft living while these things were unavailable in Sparta later proved alarmingly susceptible to the charms of both when they encountered them on their travels abroad. Perhaps the Aleuadae were counting on this, for almost as soon as payment was given to the Spartan king, someone made public the information that the king had been bribed. A brisk search of the royal tent revealed a glove packed solid with gold.

This gave the Ephors all the excuse they needed to recall their army and its errant king to Sparta, where Leotychides was prosecuted for bribery. In terms of Sparta's image with the rest of Greece, having a king arraigned on criminal charges was bad enough. Having a king executed or imprisoned would be even more of a public relations disaster. No Spartan wanted a trial in which the wrong-doings of the Spartan king would be spotlighted for an attentive world to see, still less the responsibility of deciding what to do with Leotychides if he were found guilty. So it is perhaps unfair to blame lax Spartan security for allowing Leotychides to flee to safety to Tegea, where he took shelter in a temple to Athena. Once their king was out of the way, the Spartans resolved that he could remain so, and formally exiled him.

Leotychides was thus deposed and died peacefully in exile around a decade later, while in Sparta his grandson became king in his place. By way of further reproof, after Leotychides' ignominious departure from Sparta, his home was burned to the ground with due ceremony. Less formally, but equally certainly, the king's policy of spreading Spartan dominance north of the Peloponnese went up in flames as well.

From the point of view of the Spartan Ephors and their supporters, once Leotychides – and his vision of Sparta – was out of the way, the situation stood at one down, one to go. All eyes now turned to Pausanias, whose conduct had not been doing his cause any favours.

Chapter 3

The Misadventures of Pausanias

For Pausanias, regent of Sparta, the Persian Wars were as much an image-booster for him personally as they were for his nation as a whole. As *strategos*, the general in overall command, Pausanias could claim credit for the victories at Plataea and Mycale which had effectively removed the Persians from Greek soil. No matter that Mycale had actually been won by his colleague and rival king Leotychides, or that at Plataea, where Pausanias had personally been in command, he had so comprehensively bungled his deployments that only the stubborn bravery of individual Spartan hoplites had won the day. The fact remained that Pausanias had been in command when the Greeks won their victories, so much of the credit for these victories was reflected on to him.

In fact, anyone who did not believe that Pausanias was responsible for these victories had only to listen to the man himself (if he were to permit the listener into his company), for Pausanias now began to act as though he and he alone had liberated Greece. This attitude began to grate more than somewhat with the other allied Greek states who had also played a significant part in the victory. The attitude must have been due to personal vanity, for it made terrible politics. It was not long before Pausanias had alienated not only the Greek allies, but even his fellow Spartans. The Spartan leadership, especially the Ephors, proved sympathetic to the desire of the allies for a new leader, and recalled Pausanias – something they did all the more willingly since they naturally preferred their monarchs (and regents) at home in Sparta.

However, Pausanias did not long remain in Sparta, for it became plain that if the regent were not in command of the Hellenic League, then leadership would pass to one of the more energetic and politically adept Athenians. The Ephors would prefer that the war with Persia be allowed to fizzle out, and for the allies thereafter to quietly disband the League. That was very unlikely to happen under an Athenian leader, so the Spartans reluctantly sent Pausanias to 'resume' command.

Given the boost that leadership of the Greeks gave to Pausanias' ego, it is unsurprising that he was eager to return to his position. He was also the leading proponent of the faction which wanted to maintain Sparta's leadership over the Greek alliance, and in the process convert the cities of the Aegean islands and Ionian coastline into Spartan clients. The problem was that Pausanias acted as though the Greeks were already subordinates of Sparta, and his arrogance and high-handed conduct continued to irritate the allies.

A major bone of contention was that when the Greeks had captured the city of Byzantium, several kinsmen of the Persian king had fallen into their power along with high-ranking Persian officials. Pausanias had been near Cyprus when he heard the news, and promptly proceeded to Byzantium at high speed. What happened next is contentious. According to Pausanias, these valuable prisoners had escaped from custody soon after his arrival. According to everyone else, Pausanias had arranged for the prisoners to be released so that he might then gain favour with the Persian king.

It appears that this strategy paid off, for the Persian king wrote to Pausanias:

> King Xerxes to Pausanias. I am well pleased, and my house is obliged to you for saving those persons from Byzantium. Should you wish to boldly promote both my cause and your own together, you shall not want for gold nor silver, nor troops nor ships, wherever you need them. Neither night nor day should stop you from fulfilling the promise you have shown to me. I am sending you a trustworthy man, Artabazus, with whom you can collaborate in our joint interest.
>
> (Thucydides, *The Peloponnesian War*, 1.128)

According to the enemies of Pausanias, the general had become disillusioned with his native city and the Greek allies. As a result of his earlier recall to Sparta, he had now become an out-and-out traitor. This letter from Xerxes was allegedly the response to an offer which Pausanias sent to the Persian king along with the escapees. In this offer the general proposed to turn renegade and betray the Greek cause in return for afterwards being made the Persian governor of Greece.

Exactly how Pausanias could deliver Greece to the Persians is uncertain. The Athenians only followed Spartan leadership when it suited them, and the Thebans and island cities of the Aegean were certainly sceptical. Also, if it seemed that Pausanias was planning to hand them back to the Persians, the Ionian cities would not only abandon the Spartan regent, but would probably lynch him into the bargain.

Therefore there is room for a more charitable interpretation, namely that the freeing of the prisoners was a gambit by which Pausanias planned to persuade the Persians to allow dominance of the Ionian cities by Sparta. Pausanias may even have proposed a nominal submission to the Persians in exchange for actual control, although how he could possibly have planned to sell that idea at home is hard to imagine. Nevertheless, it is possible to see how, even if mistakenly, Pausanias felt that Sparta might accept colluding with Persia if doing so would bring Ionia under Spartan control. After all, the record shows that the Spartans could be ruthlessly pragmatic in pursuit of their own interests. On the Persian side, nominal overlordship of Ionia would certainly allow Xerxes a valuable propaganda victory in the rest of his fraying empire, so we can see why he would respond positively to such an initiative. If the whole proposal still seems improbable, let us remember that a generation later the Spartans were certainly happy to accept ship-loads of Persian silver to help them conquer a fellow Greek city.

According to Thucydides, once Pausanias had received a favourable response from the Persian king, he immediately started to accustom his fellow Greeks to the idea of more Persia in their lives:

> After he had received this letter, Pausanias began to act with even more pride than he had hitherto displayed as the hero of Plataea. He no longer lived in the usual manner, but when he left Byzantium it was in Persian dress. On his travels through Thrace he was accompanied by Medes and Egyptians as bodyguards. He ate Persian-style and in many little things betrayed his ambitions on the grander scale.
>
> He became so violent that no one at all wanted to come near him, even if he had not already made access to his person difficult ... When complaints about this conduct reached the Lacedaemonians, he [Pausanias] was recalled. (Thucydides, *The Peloponnesian War*, 1.128)

Thus Pausanias was promptly yanked once more from his position of command and ordered back to Sparta, where he would become little more than mentor to his cousin, the actual, though still under-aged, king for whom he was regent.

In this and for what happened next we are fortunate to have the guidance of the near-contemporary Thucydides, one of the greatest historians of the ancient world. It should be noted, however, that in his pre-historian career Thucydides was an Athenian general at war with the Spartans. Despite his best attempts to be impartial it is probable that a degree of

anti-Spartan sentiment seeped into his work. Therefore we can legitimately be sceptical of the picture Thucydides paints of Pausanias as a
whole-heartedly traitorous villain. However, because of the way that the
political struggle played out in Sparta, the Spartans were happy to go
along with this interpretation, and indeed may have inspired it. Portraying
Pausanias as an anti-Greek traitor had the advantage of a clear narrative,
and neatly obscured the fact that in collaborating with the Persians
Pausanias might have seen himself as working for Sparta against the rest of
Greece.

Whatever doubts his narrative might raise, the account we have in
Thucydides is the only version giving more than the bare bones of events.
Therefore it is the narrative we are constrained to follow, albeit accompanied by a healthy grain or two of salt. Thucydides himself remarks that
the Spartans had no proof that Pausanias was up to anything treasonable,
and because he was Sparta's acting king Pausanias was in a position where
suspicion was not enough to bring him down. Nevertheless, the man had
shown a disturbing contempt for Sparta's near-sacred traditions, and an
unhealthy attachment to barbarian customs.

It did not help that, once it became clear that the Spartans had no
evidence which might permit them to keep holding him in Laconia,
Pausanias set off immediately for Asia Minor once more. He returned to
Byzantium, where the Athenians made it very clear that he was not
welcome. When Pausanias refused to leave quietly, he was ejected from
the city by military force. Still Pausanias did not return to his native kingdom. Instead he settled down in the nearby city of Colonae and began a
busy diplomatic correspondence with the Persians. This was too much for
the Ephors who sent an official messenger ordering Pausanias either to
come home or be considered an enemy of the state.

Accordingly Pausanias returned. It may be that he did so in the arrogant
– and possibly correct – belief that he had done nothing wrong in planning to abandon the Greek allies to the Persians in order to secure a better
position for Sparta in Asia Minor. It may also be, as Thucydides suggests,
that Pausanias had a darker motive in returning – namely that he had
decided he could get no further with the political obstruction of his
enemies at home, and had decided to overthrow the entire system.

Any enemy of the Spartans did not have to look far to discover that
nation's weak spot, and certainly not Pausanias, an insider who knew the
system intimately. Accordingly it was not long before loyal helots (or
traitorous helots, depending on one's point of view) began to pass on to

the Ephors rumours that Pausanias had been sounding them out for support should he attempt a coup. Even with the evidence slowly accumulating, it was not in the cautious and deliberate nature of the Spartan authorities to take precipitate action. Thus even at this point, Pausanias might have remained at large had not one of his confidants made a troubling discovery.

This man had been commissioned by Pausanias to carry confidential messages to the Persians. Having observed with disquiet that none of the previous messengers who had carried possibly compromising letters to Persia had returned to Sparta, he decided to take a peek at the contents of the message he had been charged with delivering. Sure enough, in a postscript Pausanias had recommended the speedy execution of the bearer.

The messenger promptly asked Pausanias to see him, and frankly admitted that he had opened the letter. He asked Pausanias if his conspiracies with the Persian king merited the death of a trusted helper, and asked about some of the details in the letter. Pausanias managed to explain away most of the messenger's fears, but in doing so made it plain that he was indeed the letter's author. This was enough to put to rest the final reservations of those Ephors who had listened to the entire conversation from behind a partition which the messenger had set up in the room.

The plan was to arrest Pausanias in the street, but the general was either forewarned by a friend or simply alerted by the demeanour of those approaching him. He immediately fled for sanctuary in a nearby temple of Athena. As a god-fearing people, the Spartans were certainly not going to wrench a supplicant out of the temple of the Goddess. Pausanias was secure in the temple *cella* – a small room within the temple precinct – and made it plain he was not going to leave voluntarily. According to the historian Diodorus Siculus, the Spartans were now forced to take the only step open to members of a warrior nation. They called in Pausanias' mother. Once this lady had been brought up to speed with events, she allegedly spoke not a word. Instead she picked up a brick, laid it across the door of the *cella*, and returned home. Taking the hint, the Spartans proceeded to brick up the only door to the windowless room. Then they themselves returned home, there to work out how long it would take a man to die of thirst and starvation.

This needed to be a precise calculation, for it would be a terrible profanation of the temple were a man to actually die within the precinct. Therefore, when it was reckoned (correctly, as it transpired) that Pausanias would be on the point of death, the door was broken down and the general was helped into the street, there to die in the open air. His death went unmourned.

> Not only did [Pausanias] fail to maintain his previous high reputation, but he ruined it through being corrupted by Persian wealth. Inflated by his own success, he had come to despise his Spartan upbringing, and was enslaved by the debauched luxury of Persia. (Diodorus Siculus, 2.46)

The end of Pausanias also sealed the fate of his Athenian colleague Themistocles. The pair had always worked so closely together in the past that it was assumed by the Athenians that if Pausanias was guilty, then Themistocles must also be a traitor. Impeached by the Athenians, Themistocles fled into exile, first to Arcadia but ultimately taking shelter with the Persian king – which in the eyes of his enemies proved that the allegations had been true all along. However, it may also be – as Plutarch, among others, suggests – that the Spartans nursed a vindictive grudge against Themistocles for his cunning refortification of Athens, and had carefully salted the evidence that they passed along to the Athenians. In which case the allegation that Themistocles was siding with the Persians was itself the reason why he was forced to do so.

Whatever the circumstances, Pausanias' demise had far wider implications than simply the death of a would-be despot and the exile of an Athenian politician. For with Pausanias died the project of bringing the Ionian cities under Spartan hegemony. So discredited was Pausanias by the manner of his death that no Spartan was ready to pick up his idea afterwards. Thereafter, Spartan involvement in the war against Persia effectively ceased. This left the Athenians free to take up the mantle of leadership in Ionia and the Aegean. With Themistocles gone, that leadership fell to Cimon, son of a famous general, and himself one of the victors of the battle of Eurymedon in 466 BC – the battle which had seen the final destruction of the Persian fleet. Cimon was one of the new generation of Athenians – possessed of boundless confidence and ambition, expansionist, adventurously opportunistic and no friend of Sparta.

Thus the Spartan attempt to capitalize on the gains from the Persian Wars came to an ignominious end. The policy of domination of northern Greece espoused by Leotychides had failed, sabotaged partly by the king's flawed strategic vision and partly by the inward-looking conservatism of the Ephors. The character of Pausanias had been a major factor in the failure of the Ionian project, but the failure of Sparta's regent could not but reflect badly on the state itself.

The wild policy swings and vacillations caused by the differing visions of Leotychides, Pausanias and the Ephors had irritated and confused Sparta's allies, and had meant that almost nothing had been done in the war against Persia. The universally high regard in which Sparta had been held at the end of the Persian invasion had been largely dissipated within a decade. The city-states of Hellas began to consider Athens as the foremost state of Greece – although most had very mixed feelings about whether this Athenian primacy was at all a good thing.

Chapter 4

The Slide into War

The fact that the Athenian exile Themistocles, an enemy of Sparta, first sought refuge in Arcadia in the Peloponnese is itself a sign of how low Sparta's prestige had fallen. Arcadia was in Sparta's own backyard – an area supposedly well under the power of the Spartan hegemony. However, the internal struggles of various Spartan political parties, and the total failure rate in recent Spartan foreign policy initiatives had encouraged a bellicose and independent streak among the peoples of Arcadia.

With contemporary and modern historians preoccupied with the various victories of Cimon against Persia's allies, the growth of the fledgling empire of Athens and the epic development of the world's first known democracy in Athens itself, the record of events in Sparta over the next few years is neglected and obscure. Nor is the situation helped by the fact that Sparta produced no historian of its own to tell us what was happening outside Athens and its empire.

One positive development in this period was that Sparta appears to have pulled itself together under a single leader. This was Archidamos, the Eurypontid successor to his grandfather, the exiled Leotychides. (The father of Archidamos had died earlier, so the succession skipped a generation.) Regrettably, we have little enough information in our sources with which to form an organized biography of this Archidamos. However, after the death of Pausanias we see a steadiness and consistency in Spartan policy which strongly suggests that Archidamos kept a firm hand on the tiller of the ship of state.

This was just as well, for by now even the founder member of the Peloponnesian League – the neighbouring state of Tegea – had progressed from restlessness to outright mutiny. Again, thanks to the unwavering focus of our sources on developments in Athens, we are left with guesswork and a few scraps from Herodotus to tell us what actually happened in the Peloponnese. We do know that matters deteriorated to the point where military action was needed to rectify the Spartan position, for Herodotus, in an aside, mentions a battle of Tegea in which Argos fought alongside Tegea against Sparta. This was followed by a yet more epic clash of arms at an otherwise unknown place called Dipaea, and this was against 'all the Arcadians except Mantinea'.

From these scanty references we can deduce that the Argives were interested in exploiting Sparta's relative weakness, and did so by stirring up unrest among Sparta's allies. Eventually matters escalated into a military confrontation. The subsequent Spartan victory at Tegea seems to have succeeded in knocking the Argives out of the war, although most of the rest of the Arcadians went ahead anyway with a full-scale war against Sparta. The writer Isocrates must be referring to this time when he makes mention of a battle in which the Spartans were greatly outnumbered. By cross-referencing this with Herodotus – who pronounced Dipaea a Spartan heroic victory – we can deduce that at Dipaea the Spartans proved yet again that the courage and training of their hoplites made them unbeatable.

Less acclaimed, but probably more significant, is clear evidence that some slick diplomacy was happening behind the scenes. Dipaea was a victory for Sparta because two significant players were missing from the anti-Laconian alliance. One was Argos and the other was Elis, a relatively large city-state on the other side of Arcadia. Elis had recently had a democratic revolution which should have placed it in the opposing camp to the Spartans (who greatly favoured and encouraged oligarchies in those cities where they had influence). Nevertheless, Spartan relations with Elis remained friendly, and Elis stayed out of the conflict.

It is also highly likely that the reason for the absence of Mantinea from the crucial battle is because the Spartans had given this city sufficient backing to enable it to stand up to the rest of the Arcadians. The battle at Dipaea probably represents an attempt by the Arcadians to dragoon Mantinea on to their side by brute force – an attempt which the Spartans resisted on Mantinea's behalf.

How much credit should be given to Archidamos, and how much was due simply to the removal from the stage of the divisive figures of Leotychides and Pausanias is hard to guess. It can definitely be said that as a result of military victory, renewed diplomatic prowess and a cessation of internal feuding, the Spartan state had more or less recovered its balance by the year 465 BC. Indeed, so far recovered were they that the Spartans had begun to feel it necessary to slap down the Athenians, whom they considered were becoming too presumptuous for their own good – or for the good of anyone else, if it came to that.

While Sparta had been struggling for stability Athens had been going from strength to strength. The last Persian allies in northern Greece, in

Eion, had been defeated. After another successful series of campaigns in Asia Minor, the allies had then concentrated on clearing a nest of pirates from the island of Skyros, from which base the pirates had plagued shipping in the Aegean.

From the Spartan perspective, it added insult to injury that the Athenians used the spoils of these victories to further strengthen the city walls of Athens, which Sparta had not wanted rebuilt in the first place. Not only were the Athenian walls strengthened, but it was at this point that construction began on the famous 'Long Walls'. These stretched from the city of Athens to the city's port in Piraeus. Once this epic task was completed, then so long as the powerful Athenian navy controlled the nearby waters, the city of Athens was impervious to siege.

Thus protected from assault by land, the Athenians were able to cheerfully ignore Hellenic outrage and proceed with the conquest of the Chersonese in northern Greece. Here they drove out the native Greeks and replaced them with Athenian settlers. Confident that the Spartans would be able to do little other than offer sympathy to the outraged supplicants who fled to them for support, the Athenians then proceeded with an ultimately successful attempt to subjugate the island of Thasos off the coast of northern Greece. By this time there was a strong and growing sentiment in Sparta that the Athenians needed to be reminded that they could not do whatever they wanted to the rest of Greece.

The Earthquake and Aftershocks

However, before the Spartans could deal with events abroad, Sparta was shaken by an internal crisis. Literally shaken – for in 464 BC a massive earthquake caused death and devastation throughout Laconia. It is reported that in Sparta itself only five houses were left standing. Contemporary sources put the number of casualties at 20,000, though it is uncertain who was counting nor how it was possible to do so. Also there was not much time for such activities, for the earthquake was only the beginning of the crisis.

It says a lot about Sparta and its subject peoples that, after crawling out from under the rubble of his home, Archidamos' first move was not to organize disaster relief but to hastily prepare for the helot revolt that would inevitably follow – as it duly did. In fact, to the Greek mind, it was the helots who had caused the earthquake in the first place.

Poseidon, known today as the God of the Sea, presented a formidable aspect to the ancient Greeks. One of his titles was 'the Earth-shaker', for it was Poseidon who, when angered, could shake the earth like a housewife shaking out a rug. And Poseidon had been given cause for anger, because a group of helots who had somehow offended the Spartans had attempted to seek refuge in the Temple of Poseidon at Taenaron. Disregarding the God's feelings, the Spartans dragged the supplicants from the altar and executed them. The earthquake happened soon afterwards.

The helots of Laconia were quick to conclude that the gods were punishing Sparta, and immediately rose in an impromptu rebellion. With utter predictability, as soon as word of the Laconian revolt reached Messenia the helot population there also took up arms. They were joined in this rebellion by some of the *perioiki* – free peoples in Laconia who were not Spartans.

It was a bad time to be part of any isolated outpost of Spartan administrators or troops, as these were quickly wiped out by the rebels. For example, in Messenia we hear of a group of 300 Spartans caught and cut down in the Stenyclerus plain. Indeed, even the main Spartan army was having trouble getting organized thanks to the logistic chaos and loss of life caused by the earthquake. Fortunately for Sparta, the people of Mantinea now took the opportunity to repay past favours and piled in on the Spartan side. Again we have Herodotus to thank for a passing comment (Book 9, 35) which tells us that a Mantinean–Spartan alliance defeated the main rebel force at a place called Isthmus, probably late in 464 BC.

As the Messenians had done in previous years and in previous wars against the Spartans, the rebels withdrew to their stronghold of last resort at Mount Ithome. After having struggled painfully to capture this mountain in previous wars, during their time of occupation the Spartans had done their very best to destroy any fortifications on Ithome. However, they could hardly flatten the mountain itself. Mount Ithome dominates the Messenian plain and is possessed of sufficient escarpments, ravines and defiles to make it non-essential for humans to embellish its natural defences. Once safely ensconced in Ithome the rebels could hold off the formidable Spartans with relative ease. However skilled the Spartans might be on the battlefield they lacked the technical ability required for successful siegecraft.

When it came to taking fortified positions the best-qualified peoples in the known world at that time were the Persians. They had demonstrated their skills not only in their recent conquest of Athens (which is how the first Athenian walls were flattened) but also in the earlier reconquest of Ionia after the cities on the Anatolian mainland had rebelled and started the Persian Wars in the first place. The Ionians had necessarily become adept at siegecraft through experience on the receiving end and they had passed on much of their competence to the Athenians. The Athenians were quick learners and had recently demonstrated their new-found expertise on the peoples of the Chersonese and Thasos.

It occurred to the authorities in Sparta that, despite recent ill-feeling, the Spartans and Athenians were technically still allies. Therefore the Spartans could legitimately call on the Athenians and their skills for help in winkling out the Messenian rebels from Ithome. Perhaps surprisingly, when the matter came to be debated in the Athenian assembly, the strongest advocate for intervention was the Athenian leader Cimon.

Here again we might suspect the hidden hand of Archidamos behind the scenes. There is an argument to be made – and Archidamos probably made it – that Sparta was now content with mastery of the Peloponnese and had ceded its ambitions in the wider world to the Athenians. However, if the Athenians wished to pursue these ambitions without hindrance, then they would do it better with a strong Sparta at their backs. Were Sparta to be weakened, then doubtless the incipient rivalry between Corinth and Argos would break into open warfare and probably drag in Boeotia as well. Add an unstable Arcadia to the mix and the Athenians would be so busy coping with the fallout from the chaos to the south-west that their ability to expand to the east and north would be badly hamstrung. Better all round to have a secure, stable Peloponnese, and if this meant working with Sparta to suppress the Messenians, then that was in the Athenians' own best interest.

It may be that such arguments persuaded Cimon. Some Athenians – always prepared to believe the worst of their politicians – suspected that Spartan persuasion had been more pragmatic and bankable. Either way, whether persuaded through reason or hard cash, Cimon managed in his turn to get the assembly to send a force of 4,000 Athenian hoplites to join the besieging force at Ithome. Accomplishing this cost Cimon much of his political capital. Therefore it is all the more surprising that the Athenians had barely arrived and set up shop before they were abruptly informed by the Spartan authorities that their presence was no longer required and they should leave immediately.

One theory is that it had become clear to the Spartans that although they had temporarily won over the Athenian leader, the troops he had sent were not necessarily in agreement. The Spartans were anyway uncomfortable with so large a force of Athenians deep within their own jealously guarded territory, and this discomfort would have doubled if it became clear that many of the rank and file of the Athenian contingent sympathized with the plight of the helots.

However, democratically minded as the Athenians undoubtedly were, sympathy for the helots was still uncharacteristic. The Athenians had heretofore showed scant sympathy for the thousands of slaves working in horrendous conditions in their own silver mines, and certainly showed little respect for the rights of their allies in the process of turning them into subjects of their growing empire. Therefore, it is a touch irrational that they should show such empathy for the oppressed helots, although human groups throughout history have been prone to irrationality, so this cannot be entirely ruled out.

Another probability is that the Athenians, having established a military presence in Spartan territory, were making the most of it. The alarmed Spartans may have observed them busily mapping out potential supply lines and routes around defensible points, and noting the best locations for bridgeheads. On the diplomatic side, the Athenians would have been chatting with the *perioiki*, and casually inquiring about weak spots in Lacedaemonia, both geographically and politically. Certainly this is what any sensible group of military men would do if they found themselves with a chance to explore what may well in the future become hostile territory, and there are indications that such information was indeed used against Sparta later. Thus it may well be that the Spartans belatedly realized that the wealth of military intelligence they were handing to the Athenians through access to their territory more than offset any use the Athenians might be against the Messenians.

Whatever the cause of the abrupt dismissal of the Athenians, the Spartans must have known that this would be seen by their allies as a slap in the face. Athenian pride was wounded, and from this point onwards Athenian policy took a distinct anti-Spartan turn. The first casualty was Cimon himself. The Athenian *demos* considered that Cimon had been instrumental in embroiling Athens in this diplomatic humiliation, and his fall from power swiftly followed. The next year the Athenians went further and ostracised him. Cimon belonged to the aristocratic party which, while still far too democratic to appeal to the oligarchic Spartans, was still much more conservative than the extreme democrats who now came to control the assembly under the skilled statesmanship of their new leader Pericles.

It is uncertain whether it was Cimon or Pericles who accomplished the removal of the Messenians from Ithome. Certainly some sort of Athenian agreement was reached with Archidamos, who himself deserves some of the credit. Unusually for a Spartan success, the recapture of Mount Ithome was accomplished through a negotiated truce rather than by military force. We have seen that adroit diplomacy had become something of a Spartan characteristic ever since the accession of Archidamos to the throne, and certainly this outcome managed to be the least unsatisfactory resolution of the rebellion for all involved. The Messenian rebels were allowed to leave Ithome unharmed. They were resettled by the Athenians in a city they had recently conquered, Naupactos in Aetolia, on the Corinthian gulf.

This diplomatic agreement notwithstanding, relations between Athens and Sparta had definitely soured. This had a knock-on effect with the other states of Greece, which found themselves in the increasingly uncomfortable position of having to align with one or other of the two Greek powers. The Argives were the first to find themselves in this position, for the new government in Athens decided that if the Spartans did not want them, then they would find other allies in the Peloponnese. After centuries of animosity the Argives were instinctively anti-Spartan and were therefore more than happy to oblige the Athenians. Just to show the Spartans how diplomatically isolated they might become, both Athens and Argos then signed identical defensive pacts with Thessaly.

Megara, a small city-state being bullied by Corinth, then appealed to Athens for help. This was duly provided, which had the effect of temporarily moving Megara into the Athenian camp at the cost of enduring bitterness on the part of the Corinthians. Corinth had always considered Argos to be a rival, and the alliance between Athens and Argos combined with Athenian interference in Megara to push Corinth firmly on to the Spartan side.

It is uncertain how welcome this Corinthian friendship was to the Spartans. Having sorted out the Messenian rebellion, the Spartans were now in the process of undoing the damage caused by the earthquake and the subsequent war. The last thing they wanted was to be involved in a series of anti-Athenian military adventures such as those in which the Corinthians now engaged.

For example, an opportunistic Athenian expedition in the Saronic Gulf was countered by the Corinthians who allied themselves with the people of Epidaurus – an alliance probably made for the express purpose of taking on the Athenians. Rebuffed, the Athenians responded by attacking the Corinthian fleet and soundly defeating it. After this the Corinthians became involved in a military dispute the Athenians were having with the island of Aegina (which lies just off the coast from Athens). Reckoning that the Athenians had overstretched themselves with an expedition to Egypt, the Corinthians tried to boot the Athenians off Aegina, only to discover that the Athenians had greater resources than expected. This second stinging defeat made the Corinthians both more furious and all the more determined to drag Sparta into any future military confrontation with Athens.

The First Clash – Tanagra

Matters were moving in that direction anyway, for the relationship between Athens and Sparta was steadily deteriorating. The end result was a pitched battle between Athens and Sparta in Boeotia some time in the late 460s. How and why it came to this point is a matter of speculation, as we have only a somewhat unsatisfactory account in Thucydides and a totally unsatisfactory account in Diodorus. The battle took place at around the time Thucydides was born, so at least he would have been able to talk to the participants. Therefore his version is to be preferred. A modern historian, I.M. Plant, built upon the Thucydidean version in an article entitled 'The Battle of Tanagra: A Spartan Initiative?' (*Historia*, 1994: 259–74), and from all of the above sources a reconstruction of the somewhat confused motives of all the participants might be at least reasonably assumed.

The basic story is as follows. The small city-state of Phocis was involved in a spat with the equally small city-state of Doris over which of them should control the sanctuary at Delphi. Although small, Doris was not insignificant as it was assumed to be the mother-city of the Dorian people, of whom the Spartans accounted themselves the leaders. In consequence the Spartans sent a very substantial force to help the Dorians keep control of the Oracle. Having fulfilled their task, the returning Spartans found that the Athenians had blocked the passes leading back through Boeotia to the Peloponnese. While the Spartans were trying to work out what to do next, the Athenians attacked them but were defeated. The Spartans then retired home through the now-undefended passes.

There are problems with this text, not least because the 'official' story masks a seething sub-plot of intrigue. For example, why did Sparta mount a large-scale military expedition for what should have been a minor policing matter? Why did the Athenians respond so vehemently? And why did the battle take place at Tanagra, which is not obviously on the return route from Doris? Also, when the battle was over, why did the Athenians turn upon the Thebans and successfully attack them?

One hint comes from the fact that Archidamos was quietly scheming with Athenians disaffected by the Periclean democracy. It is not hard to assume that the disaffected faction was hoping to stage a Spartan-backed coup just at the moment when Sparta happened to have a large army in the vicinity. The Spartan expeditionary force was too large for a mission to Doris, but as later events proved, it was just the right size to take on the Athenians. Furthermore, there were a number of secondary objectives that the mission to Doris might achieve even if the Athenian democracy could not be overthrown.

For a start, the presence of a large Spartan force at Tanagra (not obviously on the Spartan return route, but not a bad place to wait and see how things turned out in Athens) might well force the Athenians to summon their troops back from Aegina. This would have the advantage of helping the Corinthians, who were nagging the Spartans to get the Athenians off that island. Finally, the support of a large Spartan force would encourage the Thebans, whom the Spartans were rather keen to cajole into the anti-Athenian camp. Thus, by bringing so large a force into Boeotia the Spartans were attempting to kill four birds with one stone.

This also explains the Athenians' reaction. They had automatically supported Phocis since the Spartans had taken the Dorian side, and they were irritated by the blatant support for Theban dominance of Boeotia, annoyed by the attempt to force their troops off Aegina, and incensed by Spartan plotting to overthrow their democracy. The Spartans had anticipated that the Athenians might feel that way, which is why they had brought a large army in the first place.

In the event, the Spartan expedition fulfilled none of its purposes. The inter-state dispute with Phocis was only temporarily settled in the Dorians' favour. Once the Spartans had gone, the Athenians later marched into the area and handed control of the Delphic Oracle back to Phocis. The attempt to suborn Athenian democracy failed, while the Athenian troops at Aegina stayed there and in fact forced Aegina to surrender its independence and become a tribute-paying member of the Athenian-dominated Delian League. Also, after being defeated in battle with the Spartans, the annoyed Athenians took out their bad temper on the Thebans, crushing them in a follow-up battle as an object lesson about why they should not get too friendly with Sparta.

Nevertheless, Archidamos might not have felt too distressed about how this first clash had worked out. Though casualties on both sides had been heavy, the Athenians had been defeated and given a stern warning of what they could expect if they were determined to antagonize their former ally.

The Uneasy Peace

This battle should have been the opening event in a full-scale war, but apparently neither side took it that way. Rather it was seen as a brief flare-up in an otherwise cold war, with both sides settling back into guarded hostility rather than actively engaging each other in further hostilities. This was partly because the Spartans were hesitant to go to war in any case, being naturally of a cautious disposition and with tidying up still to be done in the aftermath of the earthquake and the Messenian rebellion. The Athenians also had enough on their plates already, being mid-way through a lively little war with Corinth, a large-scale (and ultimately unsuccessful) operation in Egypt and methodical expansion in northern Greece around Thrace.

As our concern is with Sparta, we need not dwell on these Athenian initiatives other than to note that Athenian ambition caused considerable concern in Sparta and elsewhere. However, one aspect of the Egyptian campaign is worthy of attention: the Persians allegedly tried to bribe the Spartans to invade Attica as a way of getting the Athenians out of their Egyptian province. As the decades went by, the Persians were to find that timely infusions of silver to the right people were more effective in controlling the Greeks than unsubtle military interventions had been.

From our point of view, the main result of the battle of Tanagra is that it largely brought to an end a period of bad-tempered clashes. These are usually lumped together under the heading of the 'Sacred War' since the most coherent part of the conflict involved control of the Oracle at Delphi. The Athenians continued to show their displeasure with Sparta by making a series of raids on coastal cities on the Peloponnese but, as we have seen, the Spartans and the Athenians alike had enough to do without a full-scale military confrontation. Both Archidamos and Pericles were good enough diplomats to be able to disengage their cities from a war which suited neither at that particular time.

The Spartans made it clear to the Corinthians that they would not support any further military action, and the Corinthians – though far from happy – were too sensible to attempt to take on the Athenians by themselves. There matters rested, but uneasily. For a while Sparta seems to have returned to peace. One major development was the death of Pleistarchus, the son of Leonidas, for whom Pausanias had been regent. Pausanias would have been next in line, but as he was dead, Pleistonax, the mature son of Pausanias, inherited the Agaid kingship.

Meanwhile the Athenians went from strength to strength. The main aim of the Athenians was now less about fighting the Persians (the original intent of the Delian League) and more about keeping control of the cities they had brought under their control. Indeed, there may have even been a formal peace made with the Persians, the so-called 'Peace of Callias'.

It seems that there was some sort of settlement, although it has been argued that the actual peace agreement was a later fabrication. That there was a cessation of hostilities with Persia may well have been why, after the supposed date of the peace in 450 BC, there was considerable unrest among members of the League. Payments demanded by the Athenians had increased even though no actual fighting was happening. However, League membership was no longer optional. Attempts to secede were regarded as rebellions against Athens.

Through diplomacy, relentless expansion and naked force the Athenians were well on the way to becoming masters of Greece. This progress was watched with increasing uneasiness by the Spartans. When the island of Euboea 'rebelled' against Athens (probably in around 449 BC, although the exact date is uncertain), Pericles took an army to restore Athenian control. This presented the Spartans with an opportunity to put a brake on Athenian ambition and gave Pleistonax a chance to demonstrate his independence from his Eurypontid co-monarch Archidamos. Under his command a Spartan force invaded Attica, prompting a frantic burst of diplomacy between Athens and Sparta. The upshot of the deal was that the Spartans withdrew from Attica and Pericles continued with the subjugation of Euboea.

Since Sparta obtained so little from the negotiations, the Spartans suspected that Pleistonax had followed the time-dishonoured tradition of other Spartan kings and taken a heavy bribe to withdraw his army from Athenian territory. However, we need not attribute the withdrawal of the Spartan army simply to a greedy king. As we have noted, the Spartans were poor at siege warfare, and the Athenians had invested a good part of the profits of their empire in making their city siege-proof. Therefore, having got to Attica and spent a while standing around on the plain of Eleusis, it was rather uncertain what the Spartans could do next apart from admire the thoroughness with which the Athenians had fortified their city.

The situation in Messenia made the Spartans uneasy about keeping their army out of the Peloponnese for any length of time, so it was inevitable that they would eventually have to march home again, with or without a Periclean bribe. This did not stop the Spartans from laying charges against Pleistonax, and one suspects that Archidamos was not unhappy to see his co-monarch removed from the picture. Now, Archidamos could settle down unhindered to serious negotiations with Pericles.

Essentially the Athenians agreed to withdraw from those areas which they directly or indirectly controlled in the Peloponnese, and to allow

Megara back under the control of the Peloponnesian League. For obvious reasons, the Athenians retained control of Naupactus and its Messenian population. States allied to one league or the other (Delian or Peloponnesian) could not be interfered with by the other, and any disputes should go to neutral arbitration. The peace was to last the traditional generation – thirty years – but given the ill-will between Athens and Sparta, few expected it to last even half that long.

The Congress of the Allies

Thucydides goes into some detail describing how Sparta and Athens eventually moved to open war, but also gave a typically dispassionate overview of what he considered the root causes of the conflict:

> Matters came to a point where the growing strength of Athens was plain for everyone to see. The Athenians had begun to interfere in the affairs of Sparta's allies to an extent that the Spartans could no longer tolerate. They decided to put all their force into the present war [Thucydides started writing before the war ended] in order to attack Athenian power, and if possible, to break it. (Thucydides, *The Peloponnesian War*, 1.118)

In other words, this war was not the unintentional result of an escalating series of clashes. According to Thucydides, it was planned from the beginning with the conscious intent, if not to destroy Athens, then at least to smack that city back down into relative insignificance. In typically Spartan fashion, through numerous compromises, vacillations and setbacks, for the next half-century their nation ground on doggedly towards that objective.

There were, of course, a number of ostensible causes for war, though none that negotiations carried out in good faith could not have resolved. As usual the Corinthians were a major aggravating factor. Although they had earlier voted not to break the peace when Samos revolted against Athens, they were more than miffed when the Athenians decided to make a defensive treaty with the island state of Corcyra (modern Corfu). Until then Corcyra had been a non-aligned state, and the Corinthians were rather keen to conquer the place – a former Corinthian colony – and take control of its substantial fleet. The Athenians were equally keen to stop them.

The end result was a clash of navies, with the reluctant Athenians doing just enough to prevent an actual invasion of Corcyra. Annoyed with Corinth, the Athenians responded by punishing another Corinthian colony called Potidaea in the Chalcidice Peninsula. Potidaea was a member of the

Delian League (*aka* the Athenian Empire) but the Corinthians were nevertheless outraged by the treatment of their former colony, and a further armed clash followed. There was no doubt that if Sparta were to go to war with Athens, Corinth would heartily agree with the decision.

Step one for a god-fearing nation contemplating a serious war was to send to Delphi to find out where the denizens of Mount Olympus stood on the matter. The Spartans duly did so. The reply was positive. In fact, Apollo gave assurances that not only did the gods approve of the enterprise, but he himself would fight on the Spartan side.

Step two was not so much to consult the allies in the Peloponnesian League as to inform them that Sparta was going to war with Athens, and their participation was strongly encouraged. Thucydides gives us a stirring speech by the Corinthians in which a litany of past complaints were used to demonstrate the future threat posed by Athens. Persuaded by Corinthian eloquence on the one hand, and doubtless by some quiet Spartan arm-twisting behind the scenes, the great majority of League members voted for war. Clever diplomacy and Theban anger with the aftermath of Tanagra ensured that for once Thebes would be on the same side as Corinth and Sparta. However, even this powerful set of allies was not enough for the Spartans. To keep a clear conscience with their gods, the final step was to ensure that the war was a consensual affair into which Athens had entered knowingly by consciously rejecting the alternatives.

Therefore an embassy from Sparta came to Athens demanding that because of a previous sacrilege, the descendants of the perpetrators should be exiled from Athens. Since those to be ejected included Pericles, the current leader of the state, this was hardly likely to happen. Furthermore, the Athenians had an answer to hand. They argued that the Spartans should in their turn eject those responsible for the 'Curse of Taenaron' – that impious slaying of helot suppliants to Poseidon which had caused the earthquake and Messenian rebellion. The walling-up of Pausanias in the temple precinct (*see* p. 25) was also brought up, with the suggestion that the Ephors should exile themselves for their role in this affair.

The Spartans tried again. This time they complained on behalf of their ally Megara. Because of a dispute with the Athenians, Megaran ships and traders had been excluded from all ports controlled by the Athenian League. The Spartans demanded that the merchants of Megara should again be allowed access to Athenian-controlled ports. The Athenians refused, but offered to let a neutral party arbitrate, as agreed by the treaty between the two states.

A third Spartan embassy arrived in Athens. This time the message from the ambassadors was definitely laconic: 'Sparta wants peace. Stop oppressing other Greeks, and peace will happen.'

By now it was clear to the Athenians that the Spartans were not trying to resolve individual issues but were looking for something they could legitimately demand of the Athenians that the Athenians did not want to give. As a speaker to the Athenian assembly correctly pointed out. 'We would not be going to war over whether to rescind the Megarean Decree. That's a minor matter. But if we were to concede and back down on this point, the Spartans will simply return with a greater demand.'

This was almost certainly correct. The Spartans had determined on war and they would keep pushing until the Athenians agreed to fight. Not that the ambitious and bellicose Athenians were averse to taking on Sparta – after all, they had already taken on mighty Persia and come out on top. Thucydides has Pericles give a detailed account of Athenian resources and possible strategies. The conclusion was that a war with Sparta would be difficult and challenging but certainly winnable.

Accordingly the Spartan ambassadors were told that Athens had no intention of backing down, but they were ready to submit any and all points of disagreement to arbitration, when and wherever the Spartans chose. On hearing this, the ambassadors left Athens without giving any reply. While no formal declaration of war had been issued, both sides now knew with certainty that conflict was inevitable. The 'Thirty Years Peace' had lasted just over half that time.

Chapter 5

The Archidamian War

Anyone familiar with Spartan history will not be surprised by what happened next. In 743 BC, when the Spartans were planning their conquest of Messenia, they first sent embassies with intolerable demands. When these demands were not met, the embassy went away without responding to the Messenian suggestion of arbitration. Then, without warning, they attacked and seized the border town of Ampheia, thus securing a crucial bottleneck in the route between Messenia and Laconia.

Fast forward to 431 BC, and the war began with a surprise attack on Plataea, a town that was a crucial bottleneck on the route between Athens and Sparta. As with Ampheia, the attack was made all the easier because the inhabitants of the town innocently believed that they were still at peace and so were not taking the usual wartime precautions. The crucial difference was that because Sparta did not share a border with Athens, the attack on Plataea was made by Sparta's allies, the Thebans, rather than by Sparta itself.

This was important because at Ampheia the Spartans had decided that if they were going to break the rules of war, they might as well break them comprehensively. They therefore assaulted Ampheia with a large force and most of the townspeople were massacred before they even knew their nation was at war. The Thebans were more squeamish:

> They were determined to be conciliatory, and if possible to reach an amicable agreement with the citizens. They ordered a herald to proclaim that any who wanted to rejoin the Theban confederacy [Plataea had once been closely allied with Thebes] should muster with their troops in the market-place. They genuinely thought that the people of the city would be happy to join them.
>
> (Thucydides, *The Peloponnesian War*, 2.2.4)

This was a serious and fatal mistake. Whatever their previous ties to Thebes, the Plataeans had stood with the Athenians throughout the tribulations of the Persian invasion, and they were not about to betray their trust lightly. Noting how small the occupying force of Thebans actually was, the Plataeans quickly and secretly mustered and then attacked and massacred their would-be allies.

For the present, Plataea was to remain an inconvenient road-block for the movement of Peloponnesian armies. However, if the attack on the city achieved nothing else, such a flagrant Peloponnesian violation of the treaty served as a declaration that the war had now officially begun. The dating of this, the most epic of Sparta's many wars, is more than somewhat confused. The reason is that the Peloponnesian War comprised not a single prolonged conflict but rather a series of wars, interspersed with fairly long periods of peace. In fact, by some counts the Peloponnesian War was already well under way. This is the argument of those who maintain it started in the late 460s with the Sacred War and the battle of Tanagra.

This is reasonable enough, as the main reason why the next two wars are counted as one is simply because the historian Thucydides decided to put them together. So masterful was his history of these conflicts that most subsequent historians have followed his example. However, the Archidamian War of 431–421 BC was a very different war from the final round of warfare which happened between 413 and 404 BC.

In his history Thucydides has Pericles give the Athenians a detailed description of the city's resources and the strategy that Athens would use to contain Sparta. Basically, the plan was as follows. There would be no attempt to engage the Spartans in Attica, even if they invaded and occupied Athenian territory. Instead, the Athenians would retreat behind their secure fortifications and supply their city from the sea. While the Spartans were unprofitably occupying themselves and rural Attica, the Athenians would continue with their expansion in the Greek north-east and slowly isolate the Spartans on the Peloponnese. While the Athenians could continue to trade profitably with their empire and the rest of the world, their navy would slowly strangle the Peloponnese – something that would be slow to affect the largely agricultural Spartans, but which would quickly cause pain to commercial states such as Corinth and Megara. Most importantly, all that Athens had to do to win the war was to endure. It was up to the Spartans and their allies to make a dent in Athenian power.

The opening stage of the war happened exactly as predicted: the Spartans put Plataea under siege and then worked around this city and Oenoe (another inconvenient obstacle) and eventually invaded Attica. In anticipation of the Spartan arrival, the rural population of Attica had evacuated themselves and everything of value to within the walls of Athens itself. This left the Spartans with the immensely difficult task of devastating what was left.

Modern archaeology has shown that it takes a lot of work to properly devastate an area. It is not enough, for example, to flatten a farmhouse if you leave the blocks of stone handy for the returning farmer to put back up. Also, it is as hard to destroy the foundations of a building as it is to put them there in the first place. Therefore, given the lack of time that devastators can spend on each building, the farmer usually has a solid base on which to begin reconstruction – especially as hard-to-replace items such as door hinges were carefully buried elsewhere on the property beforehand. We are told explicitly that evacuated farmers took with them items such as window frames, while livestock was evacuated to the nearby island of Euboea and repatriated each year after the Spartans withdrew.

The durability of an olive tree makes it hard to devastate. The tree views being cut down as a drastic form of pruning and rapidly grows back even more bushy than before. To destroy a mature olive tree one must grub it up by the roots, which is a morning's work for a squad of men, and not really practicable in all the olive groves of Attica. In the case of crops, trampling winter wheat into the soil certainly destroys the crop, but it fertilizes the ground to promote an excellent future harvest – and in any case the Athenians could import more grain from the fields around the Black Sea.

In addition, it was not as if the hoplites of the Spartan army could roll up their sleeves and settle down to the unaccustomed labour of destruction. The Thessalians still bore a grudge against the Spartans and were allied with the Athenians, and their northern state produced excellent cavalry. Both Athenian and Thessalian cavalry squads patrolled the Attic countryside, constantly clashing with their Theban counterparts, and making life precarious and short for any small groups of Spartiates who wandered too far from the main army.

Therefore the invasions of Attica, while hugely inconvenient, were far from crippling. Since the Spartans could not afford to leave their army there as a permanent occupation force, their invasions were necessarily brief. There is a growing body of evidence that suggests that many Athenians managed to practise a sort of 'guerrilla agriculture' and farmed around the invasions.

Starting Badly

The war got off to a bad start for Archidamos, who was bitterly criticized for being slow to get the Spartan army onto a war footing. Many suspected that his friendship with Pericles had led him to delay in the hope that a political solution might yet be found. Then, when the Spartans and their allies finally got their act together, they hit a stumbling block as soon as they left the friendly territory of Thebes. This was the settlement of Oenoe, a little town with very big walls, for it occupied a crucial pass in the Cithaeron mountain chain that lies between Attica and Boeotia.

The Athenians had expected the Spartans to come this way and Oenoe was garrisoned and fortified accordingly. The Spartans had previously shown their inability to conduct a decent siege, and now their army spent an inordinate amount of time proving that this was still the case. There were those who felt that Archidamos was deliberately delaying in the vain hope that the presence of an army poised to swoop down on Attica would itself be enough to bring the Athenians to terms.

The usual Spartan war had a simple strategy. One marched an army into hostile territory and proceeded to damage it until the outraged natives came out with their army to stop it. The Spartans would then beat up that army, and everyone would sit down to discuss terms. In fact, Thucydides has Archidamos state this plan explicitly:

> They will come out and challenge us when they see us destroying their property. People are outraged when they see this happening under their noses, especially if it has never happened before. Without considering the consequences, they impulsively rush out to prevent it. The Athenians are especially likely to act this way, because they are more accustomed to damaging the lands of others than suffering such devastation themselves. (Thucydides, *The Peloponnesian War*, 2.11)

This did not happen, even though once they had worked their way around Oenoe, the Spartans duly began plundering Attica. Knowing that his friendship with Archidamos might mean that his personal property outside the walls of Athens might be left untouched, Pericles pre-empted any such Spartan propaganda move by signing over these lands to the Athenian state. The knowledge that everyone was suffering alike meant that the Athenian army – while indeed deeply agitated about what was happening outside – nevertheless watched the destruction without leaving the city walls.

This was a problem. If the Spartans had any other idea of how to go about defeating Athens, we have no record of it. Nor do we hereafter observe any signs of an organized Spartan strategy. Rather, on the Spartan side we see repeated and pointless annual invasions of Attica and a series of diverse military adventures as the city thereafter struggled to find a way through the Athenian empire's defences elsewhere.

Archidamos was a man without a plan. And things were about to get worse. It was bad enough for his one-trick strategy if the Athenian army circumvented it by staying behind the city walls. But the Athenians did much more than that. Their hoplites embarked on triremes and set off for the Peloponnese. While the Spartans and their allies stood about in smoking Attic fields, the Athenians embarked on a coastal tour of the Peloponnese, stopping at vulnerable points along the Laconian coastline to indulge in some general mayhem and arson of their own.

It was at one such point – at Methone, one of the few harbours on the southern Peloponnese – that the Athenians were prevented from capturing the port by the quick actions of a Spartan officer called Brasidas – an action that earned him the first official Spartan commendation of the war. Other locations along the route of the Athenian cruise were less fortunate. Soon Archidamos was bombarded with messages demanding his army's immediate recall.

Only now was it becoming painfully clear how large a task the Spartans had taken on. The Athenians not only had a large army and fleet, they also had a huge stock of money and materiel put aside for a war that they had long foreseen. The treasury reserve came to thousands of talents of gold and silver. With a talent weighing in at around 26kg (57lb), one talent of silver was enough to keep a warship at sea for a month. If we accept the figures given by Pericles and quoted by Thucydides, Athens already had reserves sufficient to keep a fleet of 100 ships operating for another two centuries, even without the 500 talents of income arriving annually as tribute from subject states.

Sparta, on the other hand, had very little in the way of a cash reserve, as the state relied on the Spartiates financing themselves from the profits of the Messenian holdings which were farmed on their behalf by helots. While useful, and certainly making the state self-sufficient, this economic system was not particularly helpful when it came, for example, to outfitting warships which required hard cash. Therefore, there was nothing for it but that the Spartans must take a deep breath and swallow their pride, and then – on the basis that the enemy of my enemy is my friend – they decided to ask the Persians for money:

> At the end of the summer, an embassy ... set out for Asia [Minor] with the intention of asking the Persian King to provide a subsidy, or even join the war on the Spartan side. (Thucydides, *The Peloponnesian War*, 2.67)

It must be said that the Spartans never had the same inbred antipathy to the Persians that the Athenians had. As Ionians, the Athenians identified on a visceral level with the cities conquered and ruled by Persia, and they saw the war against the Persians as something of a crusade. For the more pragmatic Spartans, the war against Persia had been about throwing the invaders out of Hellas. That had been achieved, and the Persians showed no inclination to repeat the attempt. So there was no reason why normal inter-state relations should not now be restored. Asking for help against a common enemy certainly fell into that category, so the Spartans probably felt that they were doing nothing outrageous.

Nevertheless, the Athenians were outraged. When their own diplomats learned of the embassy, they prevailed on a sympathetic Persian adminis-trator to hand over the men. The prisoners were then sent to Athens. When the ambassadors arrived ...

> That same day, without a trial and without allowing the prisoners to say a word in their own defence, the Athenians executed them all and threw their bodies into a pit.
>
> This seemed to them a reasonable action on their part, since the Spartans had been behaving in the same way. Not only Athenian, but even neutral merchantmen whom they had captured sailing around the Peloponnese were adjudged to be enemies, and all these they summarily executed and threw into pits. (Thucydides, *The Peloponnesian War*, 2.67)

The Apollo Factor

At this point things were not looking good for the Spartans. They had undertaken a war against Athens without realizing what they were getting into. The Athenians on the other hand, had carefully prepared, strategized and stockpiled materiel for just this occasion. What the Spartans would have done next is not known. Come to that, it is not known what the Athenians had in mind, for it is unlikely that so aggressive and active a people intended to wait quietly for the Spartans to tire of hitting them.

In any case, none of these potential plans came to fruition because, as he had earlier promised the Spartans, Apollo now personally joined in the war and completely changed its character. Known today as the God of art, prophecy and music (and spacecraft), Apollo also had a darker side. The Greeks knew this well. In his aspect of Smintheus, he was terrible as a plague-bearer. Apollo carried not only a lyre but also a silver bow. In *The Iliad*, Apollo was said to have shot his disease-bearing arrows into the Greek camp for nine days until the Greeks agreed to release the captured daughter of one of Apollo's priests. Now, that dreaded silver bow was turned on Athens. In fact, it could be said that Athens, with the space between its walls jam-packed with a flood of refugees and livestock from the country, was an epidemic waiting to happen. And happen it did, with apocalyptic force:

> There is no record elsewhere of the disease being as virulent or lethal as it was in Athens ... people died like flies, the bodies of the dead heaped on top of each other, while others, half dead themselves, staggered around them ... the temples were choked with the bodies of those who had sought succour in them ... The catastrophe was so overwhelming that people assumed they were condemned already and ignored the strictures of religion and law. (Thucydides, *The Peloponnesian War*, 2.50ff)

It was only a matter of time before the plague spread from Athens to the Athenian army operating in the Greek north-east, and there too it proved catastrophic. Thucydides is explicit in his description of the plague and the symptoms, and he should have known because he was himself afflicted but survived.

The best guess is that this plague was typhoid fever, which accounts for many (though not all) of the described symptoms. This suspected disease has received (disputed) confirmation from a study of a mass burial pit dating to around the time of the plague. Tooth root pulp shows the DNA of the dead was infected with something closely resembling typhoid. Because diseases can mutate rapidly, it is possible that the ancient version of typhoid also included something which produced effects resembling viral haemorrhagic fever. It is also quite possible that, thanks to the over-crowding and insanitary conditions among the population cooped up within the walls, the Athenians managed to pull off a double and have con-current epidemics of haemorrhagic fever and typhoid running rampant through their city.

As ever in such cases, no one stopped afterwards to make a tally of the dead, but the outcome was crippling. Athens lost around a third of the city's population. Lacking the manpower to do much else, the people drew back within the city walls and adopted a much more defensive posture. Whatever plans Pericles had to make life uncomfortable for Sparta are unknown. These plans, like Pericles himself, died in the plague.

Plataea

The Spartans observed the unusual number of funeral pyres burning in the city and correctly deduced that Apollo was at work within. Therefore they carefully withdrew their army out of range of the contagion and concentrated on reducing Plataea. The attack was led by Archidamos, who, given his fondness for diplomacy, naturally first attempted to talk the Plataeans out from behind their walls.

The initial suggestion was that Plataea should become a neutral state, and that both Athenians and Spartans should be allowed free passage through Plataean territory. This was basically all that the Spartans wanted of Plataea anyway. However, the Plataeans pointed out that their wives and children had already been evacuated to Athens, so neutrality would be hard to achieve.

Archidamos then came up with a second plan: that the Plataeans should hand over the city to the Spartans and be evacuated to a place of safety where they could sit out the war. The Spartans would make a careful record of what was handed over to them, keep it in trust and give it back when the war ended. After consulting with the Athenians, the Plataeans rejected this plan also. At this point Archidamos accepted that only force would decide the issue. He gave the Plataean ambassadors a short speech which could be summarized as saying 'On your own heads be it.'

The siege began. The Spartans started conventionally enough by heaping earth against the walls in order to build a siege mound that would enable them to swarm over the ramparts when the walls were high enough. This took a perplexingly long time. Eventually the Spartans worked out that the Plataeans had tunnelled through their own walls, and were removing earth from the bottom of the mound as fast as the Spartans were piling it on top. Furthermore, the Plataeans were adroit builders and when the Spartans started packing the earth in baskets to make it harder to remove, the Plataeans concentrated instead on making the wall next to the mound even higher. Consequently, even when the siege mound had reached an impressive height, it was still more or less at ground level relative to the ramparts above it.

Just to make doubly sure, the Plataeans also built a second crescent wall behind the ramparts. Therefore even if the Spartans got over the first wall, they would find a second wall waiting for them to build another siege mound alongside, albeit in a position exposed to missile fire on the flanks. The Plataeans made it plain they were prepared to build a succession of such walls in a line right across the city, if the Spartans really wanted to go that way.

Giving up on the mound, the Spartans tried battering rams and other siege engines. The Plataeans had anticipated that the Spartans would try this and had built swings to counter the machines. The upper part of these swings overhung the city walls and swung parallel to them. At the bottom of each swing was a large and heavy log. When the Spartan war engines approached the walls, the logs were pulled back and allowed to swing down. The length of the chain was calculated so that the bottom of the swing was a few feet above the ground. At that height, and moving at the fastest point in its arc, the blunt end of the log smashed into the siege engine. This did to the engine what the ram was supposed to do to the walls, but with considerably more effect.

With conventional forms of attack exhausted, the Spartans were forced to move out of their comfort zone and innovate. They noted that the city was not especially large, and an intense fire might carry within the walls and save the Spartans the effort of burning the place down afterwards. Accordingly, huge heaps of firewood were loaded against one wall, with the direction selected in accordance with a promising wind that was picking up. The wood was steeped in pitch, and sulphur was added to make for a truly hellish burn. Indeed, the plan might have succeeded, so intense was the fire. Regrettably, that freshening wind was the harbinger of an approaching thunderstorm and the subsequent deluge dampened both the fire and the Spartan resolution to bring the siege to a quick conclusion.

Accordingly, the Spartans settled on the tried-and-trusted method of ancient siege warfare. They built a wall of their own around the city so that the defenders could not get out even if they wanted to. Then they sent away the greater part of the army while the rest settled down to see how long it would take before the Plataeans ran out of food. (*See* R.C. Blockley, 'Dexippus and Priscus and the Thucydidean Account of the Siege of Plataea', *Phoenix*, 1972 (26): 18–27.)

The War Drags On

The war began to assume a pattern. The Athenians refused to challenge the Spartans to a direct battle, but they continually picked away at Sparta's allies in the north, here raiding a tribe north of the Corinthian Gulf, there capturing a city in Thrace which was aligned with the Peloponnesian League. Since these small wars were far from Sparta's borders, the only way to get there quickly was by ship, and to do this the Peloponnesians had first to get past the formidable Athenian navy. Several early actions quickly demonstrated to the allies that the Athenians were by far their masters at sea. Even when considerably outnumbered the Athenians showed a distressing tendency both to seek battle and to emerge victorious thereafter.

The Spartans did make one daring raid, inspired by Brasidas, that same officer who had been commended for his defence of Methone. Having been defeated in a sea battle near Corinth, Brasidas came up with the idea of ordering his rowers to carry their oars across the peninsula to crew some old ships which were in reserve on the eastern shore. The original idea was to row these ships swiftly across the Saronic Gulf and make a surprise raid on Piraeus itself. (The Athenians were so secure in their mastery of the sea that it had never occurred to them to secure their port.)

This daring plan failed, partly because some of the Peloponnesian leaders baulked at tweaking the tail of the Athenian lion in its own den, and partly because the reserve ships were elderly, leaky vessels. This would make escape difficult for those fleeing the scene of the crime, especially as one might reasonably expect a number of sleek and vengeful Athenian triremes in pursuit. In the end the raiders chose the more vulnerable depot at Salamis as their target. The attack caused huge uproar and panic in Athens, and the Peloponnesians managed to escape safely with plunder and three captured ships.

Brasidas was rapidly making a name for himself in Sparta, a nation unaccustomed to its commanders thinking unconventionally. New ideas were needed, since it was becoming plain that this war could not be finished quickly, and conventional options were increasingly limited. The Athenians seemed to have an unlimited supply of ships (at this point there were some 250 of them operating in different theatres) and this made it very difficult for the Spartans to conduct operations anywhere. Another annoyance was that Sparta's allies seemed to regard their role as having been to drag Sparta into war with the Athenians. This accomplished, they considered their part done and largely sat back and waited for the Spartans to get on with things.

A good example of this attitude was the revolt of Mytilene, a city on the island of Lesbos near the Anatolian coast. Upset by ever-increasing Athenian demands and certain that they had joined the Delian League to fight the Persians and not the Spartans, the entire island repudiated its alliance. A delegation was sent to ask the Spartans for help. This the Spartans were eager to give, if they could only work out how. Lesbos was a long way off and there was no chance of getting there by sea. Since none of their more maritime allies was ready to help Lesbos, in the end the Spartans decided to launch an attack on Attica by land and sea in the hope of drawing Athenian attention away from the rebels.

This plan failed ignominiously. A mass attack needed both ships and the help of the allies. But the allies were busy with seasonal work in their fields and were slow to muster, while the Athenians responded quickly. Without recalling a single ship, they mustered a further fleet from their reserves and were eagerly patrolling off the isthmus before the Peloponnesians could get their invasion fleet out of the docks. The combined assault on Attica was ended before it began and the failure of this assault meant no help for Mytilene. The city fell back into Athenian hands. The population was enslaved and the ringleaders of the rebellion executed. Even that the Athenians considered a huge concession as the original plan had been to massacre the entire population as a ghastly warning of the dangers of relying on Peloponnesian help.

Disorganized fighting continued in the north-east, and there were occasional clashes in Boeotia, but essentially the war was at a stalemate. When Archidamos died in 426, five years of war had accomplished very little other than depleting the manpower and treasuries of both sides. Nevertheless, the Athenians had to feel that their strategy was working. They were making progress in northern Greece and their empire had remained cohesive. Morale among the citizenry was high and the city's aggressive spirit undiminished.

Not so in Sparta. Agis, the Eurypontid successor to Archidamos, was still finding his feet in his new role as king. His colleague was Pleistonax (now recalled from exile) who was strongly against further military adventures. The Ephors were in agreement, so an embassy was sent to sound out the Athenians about halting the war – probably on the basis that everything should go back to the way it was before hostilities had broken out. The Athenians rejected this olive branch with such contempt that Thucydides does not even give us the exact terms the Spartans were offering.

Pylos

The Spartans did have one important success: Plataea had finally fallen into their hands. True, this capture was mainly the physical structure of the city. Most non-combatants had been evacuated beforehand, and many of the remaining defenders had staged a large-scale break-out when food began to run low. As the Athenians had done at Mytilene, the Spartans decided to make a statement with their capture of Plataea.

All their captives were asked a single question: what had they done to help the Peloponnesians in their war against Athens? Those who failed to give a satisfactory answer were killed on the spot. Then the city itself was methodically razed and a large temple complex to the Goddess Hera was raised on the site. The little city of Plataea, which had been flattened by the Persians for its loyalty to Athens in earlier wars, was now destroyed once again. (The city was rebuilt long after the war, in 386 BC, destroyed again in 373, and resurrected once more in 338. Today it is a pleasant village a short drive from Athens, with little to show for its highly eventful past.)

As the war rolled into its sixth year, the Spartans despondently noted further signs of increasing enterprise among the Athenians. Not only were they ever more involved in the complex and messy politics of northern Greece, but they had extended their reach to Sicily where they attempted to overthrow the hegemony of Syracuse, a Dorian settlement and therefore naturally aligned with the Spartans.

Two Athenian generals of very different character had come to the fore in recent years. There was Nicias, a meticulous commander, averse to risk and careful with the lives of his men. He tended to fight only when victory was certain, and then after thorough and careful planning. Demosthenes was more enterprising, opportunistic and unconventional. The Spartans preferred to fight Nicias. Nicias tended to win his engagements, but at least one knew where one stood while fighting him.

Demosthenes demonstrated his unconventional side at Pylos, on the Messenian side of the Peloponnese. Lying at the base of the most westerly of the three peninsulas that stretch from Greece into the Mediterranean, the bay behind Pylos makes it one of the few hospitable landings on an otherwise hostile shore. The island of Sphacteria just to the south creates an even larger body of sheltered water, called today the Bay of Navarino.

According to Thucydides, Demosthenes came to Pylos by accident, his ships driven there by a storm while the Athenians were on what was by now a routine stop-and-plunder tour of the Laconian coastline. This time was different, because Demosthenes realized the potential of the site and encouraged his soldiers to extend the *ad hoc* fortifications they had started to build on their own account.

Modern historians are somewhat sceptical that the occupation of Pylos was quite that spontaneous. Unless armies have changed radically over the millennia, soldiers seldom build fortifications just to while away the hours. However, it is clear that the occupation and fortification of Pylos came as almost as much of a shock to the Athenian government as it did to the Spartans, so perhaps Demosthenes had concealed his plans from his own leaders in the belief that it was easier to get their blessing for an accomplished achievement than for a theoretical plan.

That the Spartans were shocked is evident from the fact that when news reached the army, it cut short the annual commute to devastate the fields of Attica and returned home after a sojourn abroad of only fourteen days. There was good reason for their alarm. For centuries it had been Sparta's nightmare that enemies would occupy the island of Kythera, just off the Laconian coast. From there it would be easy for raiding parties to strike inland and stir up trouble with the helots and disaffected *perioiki*. That their worst enemy should establish a fortified base on the mainland, and on the Messenian coast at that, was worse even than the prospect of an enemy-occupied Kythera. Small wonder they reacted violently.

Both sides called for help. While the Spartan army rushed back from Attica, the Spartan fleet, which had been operating in western waters well away from the bulk of the Athenian navy, was summoned to Pylos. Brasidas, the best general available, was sent to help with operations. Demosthenes in his turn sent to Athens and nearby naval units urgently asking for reinforcements. Then, aware that help would be some time in coming, he prepared to stand siege on his rocky peninsula.

The Spartans decided to close off the Bay of Navarino by placing ships across the entrance to the bay on either side of the island of Sphacteria. They then put a substantial body of hoplites on the island itself and used the remainder of the troops to effect a landing on the beach of Pylos. Given the ruggedness of the peninsula, the number of possible invasion beaches was limited to just one, and that one was far from ideal. It was too narrow for more than a fraction of the army to deploy at one time. Even a lesser general than Demosthenes would have figured out that the attack would land here, and so prepared for it.

For two days the Spartans flung themselves at the makeshift walls and struggled to establish a foothold on the beach. Rebuffed on both fronts, they retired to build siege engines to aid their attack. This might have worked, but the fatal flaw in the plan was that it needed time – and time had just run out. Few sights could have been more welcome to Demosthenes than the appearance from the west of dozens of Athenian triremes, summoned from their base at Zakynthos.

After one horrified look at the approaching Athenians, the Spartans abandoned their plan to guard the entrance to the bay and withdrew their fleet into the small natural harbour formed by the Pylos peninsula and the mainland itself. The tables were thoroughly turned and it was now the Spartans on the defensive. It was too late in the day for an Athenian assault so both sides spent the night preparing for the inevitable clash on the morrow. The battle of Pylos had therefore two very distinct parts. In part one, as we have seen, the Spartans tried to defeat the Athenians and overwhelm their fortifications. In part two, the Athenians tried roughly the same thing, although there was also a substantial Spartan fleet up for grabs and the Athenians were keen to capture that too.

In the event, the Athenians failed, but it was not for lack of trying. In fact, the Athenian attackers managed to tow off several Spartan ships that had been beached at accessible points (Greek warships were run up on the nearest sandy beach when they were not in use). Spartan stubbornness and fighting ability prevented them from being overwhelmed although casualties were heavy on both sides. The end result was somewhere between a draw and a minor defeat for the Spartans. This was not enough for the Spartans who had needed a conclusive victory. The hasty withdrawal of the ships guarding the passage into the bay had left some 400 Spartan soldiers stranded on the island of Sphacteria. For reasons which will now be explained, they were men whom Sparta could not do without.

Chapter 6

Sphacteria and the Peace of Nicias

The Vanishing Spartiates

Even before the Persian Wars, Sparta had a hidden but growing problem. The nation was running out of Spartans. The reasons why this should be so have been hotly disputed by academics in a debate which has lasted considerably longer than the Peloponnesian War itself. There is no space here to examine the various theories and counter-arguments. Therefore we shall take Plutarch at his word (while accepting that there are reasons for doubting him), and look at this key passage in Plutarch's biography of a later Spartan king, Agis IV.

> A certain powerful man, Epitadeus by name, who was headstrong and of a violent temper, came to be Ephor. When he had a quarrel with his son he introduced a law permitting a man during his lifetime to give his household and kleros to anyone he wished, or to leave it to [someone] in his will. (Plutarch, *Agis IV*, 5.2*)

This was a dramatic change from the earlier situation which Plutarch had described in his *Life of Lycurgus*. Under the previous arrangement, the state lands of Sparta – including all the conquered lands of Messenia – had been divided into 9,000 lots (*kleroi*), each of which was assigned to a young Spartiate at birth once the baby had been deemed physically acceptable to the elders. (There is also an argument that the physical criteria of what constituted an acceptable Spartan baby had grown stricter over time. Thanks to infant mortality and disease, any ancient population struggled to maintain its replacement rate even without the killing of 'unsuitable' babies. In this context the Spartan habit of winnowing down the number of available children would have pushed the population into a slow downward spiral.)

The theory was that a boy was assigned the *kleros* for his lifetime and on his death it returned to the state for further allocation. While he had use of the landholding, the Spartiate's helots farmed it, and the surplus from the

* Following Stephen Hodkinson's translation in 'Land tenure and Inheritance in Classical Sparta', *Classical Quarterly*, 1986/2009 (36.2): 378–406.

landholding was used to support the Spartiate and pay his mess funds in Sparta. The mess (*syssitia*) was more than a common dining hall. It formed the centre of a Spartiate's social life, and which mess he belonged to said a lot about his wealth, tribal affiliations and social standing. Membership of a *syssitia* was also an essential qualification for membership of the so-called 'equals' – the Spartiate rank of society. It followed that a Spartan without a *kleros* was a Spartan without Spartiate rank. Over the course of time, this fact was literally to be the downfall of Sparta.

It is probable, given the way that human nature works, that the change forced through by Epitadeus seemed a minor matter at the time. Given that a Spartan relied on the surplus from his landholding for his social standing, he would naturally be interested in getting the maximum return from the property, which in turn required investment in livestock, farm buildings and so on. Once a Spartiate had put in that effort, he would want the land reallocated to his son after his death. It would be unfair for it to go to a stranger while his son inherited a less well-developed landholding. Therefore it is quite probable that some *kleroi* had been in the same family for generations before Epitadeus made the process official.

The key issue, though, lay in the words which declared that a kleros could be given by the landowner to 'anyone he wished'. Up to this point we have no idea of the situation with regard to property rights for women in Sparta. It is quite probable – and hints in the sources confirm this – that women were already able to hold property, given the relatively enlightened Spartan attitude to women's rights. After the changes by Epitadeus, women were also now able to inherit *kleroi*.

In later texts we see that Spartan women were aggressively hypergamous (that is, they tried hard to marry men of higher social standing and wealth than themselves) and there is no reason to assume that this was a new development. Spartan women were always explicitly encouraged by the state to make the best possible match for themselves. As has been shown by modern computer simulations, the result of these tendencies combined with a low birthrate to produce a social pathology by which land was steadily concentrated into fewer and fewer hands. That is, a woman holding five *kleroi* might marry a man with ten *kleroi*, inherit both (Spartan women tended to outlive their men) and pass to her son lands which once might have supported fifteen Spartiates (*see* T. Figueira, 'Population Patterns in Late Archaic and Classical Sparta', *Transactions of the American Philological Association*, 1974 (116): 165–213).

The result of this process was that fewer and fewer Spartans actually attained the property ranking required to become a Spartiate. The lower-ranking citizens were naturally more than somewhat dissatisfied with their lot, and the number of Spartiate hoplites was dropping fast. Since the people who were required to reverse this decline were the very ones who benefited most from it (i.e. the landholding elite), a certain degree of wilful blindness to the problem might be expected. Certainly by the time reforms were eventually contemplated it was far too late. Over a century before Sparta's fall, Aristotle observed that 'Although the country is capable of supporting fifteen hundred cavalry and thirty thousand heavy-armed troopers, they [the Spartiates] number not even a thousand' (Aristotle, *Politics*, 1265) – and that number would keep dropping.

All the above is highly speculative, although perhaps the most convincing of several theories which have been advanced. We have no further information about Epitadeus, and given the innate secrecy of Spartan affairs and their lack of historians, we do not know when this change took place (or even know for certain that it did). What we do know is that by the time of the Peloponnesian War the number of Spartiates was in precipitate decline. Consequently the Spartiates trapped on Sphacteria had a significance much higher than their actual number. They belonged to members of the top families in the state and the Spartans were desperate to get them back.

The Siege of Sphacteria

The Athenians were well aware of the value of the men they had trapped and hoped to drive a hard bargain. They knew that there was already considerable sentiment for ending the war on the Spartan side, and the threat of losing more of their prized manpower would encourage the Spartans to make further concessions. Offering as security the ships trapped in the harbour of Pylos, the Spartans arranged a ceasefire until a full peace could be agreed with the Athenian assembly.

Rather perfidiously, when news came that the assembly had rejected the peace proposal, the Athenians kept the Spartan ships, claiming that the Spartans had been guilty of numerous minor breaches of the ceasefire while their ambassadors had been away. From the Spartan point of view, the only good thing about the delay was that it had allowed them to establish a tenuous supply line. Sphacteria was very close to the Messenian mainland and a strong swimmer could make the crossing at night carrying with him a limited amount of supplies. The Spartans offered large monetary rewards to anyone who would make the attempt. Enough helots and free citizens volunteered for the perilous crossing for the hoplites on the island to eke out a precarious existence.

The question of supplies also affected the enemy. Pylos was itself infertile, which was not a problem for the Athenians as long as they could be resupplied by sea. But the season was closing fast, and soon winter storms would make the notoriously dangerous southern Peloponnese coast impassable to shipping.

At this point the Athenian leader Kleon came out to personally oversee operations. He had been instrumental in rejecting the Spartan terms and stood to lose much personal prestige if the siege of Sphacteria ended ignominiously without any benefit to the Athenians. The Spartans looked quite capable of standing siege until winter. This left as the only option a direct assault – and no one was particularly looking forward to that. The prospect of facing several hundred of the best warriors in the known world, fighting desperately for survival from a highly defensible position, would have given pause to even the bravest Athenian hoplite. Therefore the Athenians did what the Athenians did best – they improvised.

First, either deliberately or by accident, Athenian sailors lit a fire on the island, denuding it of vegetation and thus cover for the defenders. Then in a surprise attack, Demosthenes gained a foothold on the island and landed a substantial number of troops. In an innovative move, he deployed more light skirmishers than hoplites. Demosthenes did not have a traditional infantry clash in mind. The Spartans were without skirmishers of their own, either because they had not landed any when they first occupied the island or because these more lightly armoured troops had quickly worked out that if food was being carried to the island by midnight swimmers, it was possible for them to depart in the same manner.

This lack of missile troops proved a fatal weakness for the beleaguered Spartan hoplites. Every time they tried to close with the skirmishers, the Athenians skipped away, flowed around to their flanks and rear and continued to bombard them with missiles:

> The Athenian light troops let fly with arrows, spears, stones and whatever else they could hurl. The Spartans were thrown into confusion because they were not used to this kind of fighting ... They had no means of striking back, and were unable to either defend themselves nor escape. (Thucydides, *The Peloponnesian War*, 4.34)

The end came when the Spartans finally found a position with secure flanks and hunkered down, only to have the Athenians bring up bowmen on the front and rear and launch a continual hail of arrows. It was clear that not only were the Spartans doomed to defeat, but they would be wiped out while they had barely landed a blow on their opponents. Unsurprisingly, when Kleon and Demosthenes offered to stop the fighting and negotiate, the Spartans enthusiastically accepted. After an exchange of ambassadors, a messenger from the Spartan authorities told the men on the island, 'Do what you want, but do not do anything dishonourable.' After some contemplation, the Spartans on the island decided that, although unprecedented, under the current circumstances surrender was not dishonourable. Accordingly, Kleon returned to Athens with 292 prisoners, of whom 120 were Spartiates.

While Pylos was a worthwhile military victory, the propaganda victory was even more substantial. Until then, the rest of Greece had taken it for granted that Spartans would fight to the death no matter what the circumstances. That they might surrender made them so much more human that one Athenian asked his prisoner if the 'real' Spartans were those who had died fighting. The irritable reply was, 'Those would be valuable arrows you have, that could kill the brave men and spare the rest.' Nevertheless, it was at Pylos that the illusion of Spartan invincibility was shattered. Thereafter the rest of Greece operated on the assumption that the Spartans could be beaten – the challenge was only to figure out the best way to do it.

Advantage Athens

With valuable hostages actually in their hands, the Athenians made it clear they would be merciless in making use of them. The Spartans were informed that if they invaded Attica over the coming summer, they would be able to see their captured Spartiates again – as they were taken out on to the walls and there executed one by one. This effectively put Attica off limits to the Spartans, so the war moved into the only battleground still available: northern Greece. The Spartans were averse to sending their army so far from home and indeed, they might have welcomed the excuse for staying even out of Attica, for the problem of Pylos had not gone away with the Athenians and their prisoners. The army was needed at home.

The Athenians had handed over the peninsula – and its by now rather elaborate fortifications – to the Messenians. Garrisoned by a mix of renegade helots and vengeful settlers from Naupactus, the Messenians kept the Spartan army busy by venturing from their base at unexpected intervals and attacking with a series of hit-and-run raids. In this the Messenian guerrillas were actively aided by their helot countrymen. The Spartans were unsure how to deal with this phenomenon as guerrilla wars were not their forte, and any wholesale punishment of their helot population for collaborating with the raiders risked damaging their agricultural base.

It was at this point that the Spartans perpetrated a sinister atrocity which was to remain as an enduring stain on the nation's reputation. The constant Spartan preoccupation with the helots had intensified as the war went on and the Spartans feared that the Athenians might attempt to promote another helot uprising. Accordingly, they decided to ask the helots themselves to nominate those men whom they felt had helped the Spartans most in their war effort – for example, those who had risked their lives supplying the beleaguered Spartans at Sphacteria.

Some 2,000 helots were so nominated and the Spartans announced that these men were to be given their freedom. In fact, the Spartans had wanted the helots to point out community leaders and natural leaders, assuming those were most likely to rebel. They helped the men to celebrate their freedom, which turned out to be short-lived: 'Soon afterwards the Spartans disposed of them, and no one afterwards knew where or how they died', reports Thucydides bleakly (*The Peloponnesian War*, 4.80).

Another solution was to get as many helot trouble-makers as far away as possible. This combined neatly with the Spartan unwillingness to send their army far afield. Brasidas was charged with making war with the Athenians in northern Greece, and was allowed to equip a select force of 700 helot soldiers. With these men Brasidas proceeded north, picking up further troops from his Corinthian and Boeotian allies.

The Spartan objective was to work with Perdiccas, the Macedonian king, who had been alarmed by the aggressive Athenian expansion into Thrace, his backyard. Because of this Perdiccas was more than ready to provide supplies and materiel for the Spartan expeditionary force, which rapidly became a thorn in the Athenian side. It did not help that the Athenians, knowing the main Spartan army was confined to the Peloponnese, had attempted to expand operations into Boeotia and had been handed a stinging setback by the Thebans. This defeat left the Athenians – already operating at full stretch – somewhat short of manpower.

In a major victory, Brasidas and his rag-tag army managed to take the city of Amphipolis, persuading it to surrender just before an Athenian fleet arrived to relieve the city. (Athens' loss was posterity's gain, for the Athenians were so upset with the tardy arrival of their fleet that they exiled the admiral in charge. This admiral was none other than Thucydides, who was consequently left free to settle back and write the history of the war for the edification of later generations.)

Once again Kleon opted to take charge personally. In 422, once the truce for the Pythian games had ended (the Greeks did not allow warring states to participate in athletic contests, so there tended to be a ceasefire before major sporting events), Kleon set off northwards with the intention of recapturing Amphipolis and driving the annoying Brasidas out of Thrace. The result was a pitched battle outside the walls of Amphipolis in which Kleon did indeed succeed in getting rid of Brasidas. The price for this achievement was high. Although Brasidas died in the battle, he secured a comprehensive Spartan victory with many Athenian casualties – including Kleon himself.

The Peace of Nicias

By now the war had been going on for over nine years and a degree of exhaustion had set in. The Spartans had been eager for peace for some time. They were uncomfortable with the deteriorating situation in Messenia and disliked operating abroad in northern Greece. Furthermore, those allies once eager for war were now just as eager for peace and the release of the stranglehold that the Athenian navy had put on their maritime trade.

The problem had been that while the war was going well for the Athenians, they saw little reason to stop. Now that the Spartans were no longer raiding Attica they were barely a nuisance, and until the eruption of Brasidas into the north things had been going well for the Athenians there as well. It is the opinion of Thucydides that Kleon had been one of the major impediments to peace, so his death smoothed the way for negotiations. (It is quite possible that Kleon was one of those responsible for having Thucydides removed from his command, so the historian might be excused a degree of animosity in this case. Certainly his description of Kleon seems more unflattering than the man's actual performance warrants.)

In any case, both sides were now ready for peace and a *de facto* armistice was put in place while everyone tried to work out the details. While both Brasidas and Kleon had been doing rather well out of the war, leadership had now defaulted on the Athenian side to the cautious Nicias and on the Spartan side to Pleistonax. Nicias was anxious to lock in the gains that the Athenians had already achieved, and also wanted an opportunity to rebuild the financial reserves which the war had been steadily draining away. The Spartans wanted the prisoners from Sphacteria returned and the threat from Pylos removed.

King Pleistonax also had another more personal reason for wanting peace. He had been restored to the Spartan throne, but the allegations that he had once been bribed by the Athenians had not gone away. Many pious Spartans believed that the gods themselves were offended by the king's restoration. Therefore every setback in the war, be it minor or major, was seen as another vote of divine disapproval for the current government. Pleistonax wanted peace partly to get his critics off his back.

The basic agreement was for a return to the *status quo ante bellum*. The Athenians would return Pylos and the Spartans would return Amphipolis. No one could return Plataea, because it was not there any more, but the land would remain under the control of Thebes. Delphi was to become autonomous, thus resolving an issue that had been rumbling along in the background since the 460s. The Sphacterian hostages would be allowed home. Then everyone would settle down to a peace scheduled to last for fifty years.

As it stood the peace represented a clear Athenian win. After all, the Spartans had gone to war in order to blunt the power of Athens and break up the Delian League. Yet after a decade of warfare, the Athenians still had an iron grip on their allies. A new generation was beginning to replace the casualties of the plague, so if anything Athens had come out of the war tried and tested and stronger than before. Sparta on the other hand had lost considerable prestige. The once-invincible Spartan hoplite was now seen as distinctly fallible, and the helots of Messenia had discovered new ways to discomfit their Spartan masters. Furthermore, Sparta's allies were furious when they discovered that some of the minor clauses in the peace treaty allowed the Athenians to hold on to territorial gains at their expense. However, a further clause in the treaty stipulated that Athens and Sparta would come to each other's aid if attacked (or if the helots staged another uprising), so there was little the offended Spartan allies could do at that time.

In the long run the dissatisfaction of Sparta's allies was to fatally undermine the treaty, which anyway had other flaws built in. The basic issue was that the Spartans and Athenians had disposed of matters to their own satisfaction and paid little attention to the priorities of the other parties involved in the war. For example, it turned out that the people of Amphipolis did not actually want their city given back to the Athenians, and in the face of their emphatic protests the Spartans were reluctant to hand it over. Since the Spartans were not keeping their side of that particular bargain, the Athenians decided to hold on to Pylos.

It did not help that the Athenians considered the war to have been won, and therefore their ambitions and aggressive opportunism were undiminished. Where Sparta's prestige had declined, Athenian stock had risen. Partly as a result of this, an outbreak of Athenian-style democracies cropped up in the Peloponnese. Argos also scented opportunity. The city had sat out this first round of war as a neutral. This by no means meant that the city had abandoned its long-held antipathy towards Sparta, and the Argives immediately set about exploiting their enemy's perceived weakness. A sort of unofficial alliance developed between Argos and two democratic states, Mantinea and Elis, which the Spartans had formerly considered firm allies.

Sparta also had internal problems. For a start there were the 700 helots whom Brasidas had taken north. This had seemed a good idea at the time, but now the Spartans realized they were hosting a small army of trained veteran soldiers who had no cause to love them. As a result these helots were encouraged to settle elsewhere, which they did. Most established themselves in settlements on the border with Elis, a location which did little to help Spartan relationships with that state.

Aside from the problem of what to do with the formerly oppressed helots, there was also the problem of what to do with the formerly ruling Spartiates from Sphacteria. There was a feeling that these men had in some way let Sparta down and that their commitment to the Spartan ideal could no longer be trusted. Initially moves were made to deny these men the right to hold public office, and also to place other restrictions on their participation in the state. This did not last long because the former prisoners were from well placed families which quickly used their influence to make sure that their relatives could once again participate fully in Spartan affairs. However, tensions and distrust remained high.

Athens had its own problems, chief among which was a young, charismatic, self-centred and totally amoral young politician called Alcibiades. Affronted that Nicias had excluded him from negotiations with the Spartans, Alcibiades was quite happy to undermine the peace treaty if this meant he could undermine Nicias at the same time. Consequently Alcibiades and his followers were the most vocal supporters for an alliance with Argos, not despite the fact that this was against the spirit of the treaty with Sparta, but for precisely that reason.

Alarmed by Athenian overtures to states in the Peloponnese, the Spartans renewed their alliance with Thebes. This was in contravention of the terms of the peace treaty, because the Boeotians had refused to accept this treaty and therefore made themselves inadmissible as Spartan allies. The Athenians (prompted by Alcibiades) demanded that the Spartans renounce their Theban allies and do as agreed and hand back Amphipolis. When the Spartans refused the Athenians went ahead and made a formal alliance with Argos, Mantinea and Elis.

Encouraged by this, the Argives began to harass the neighbouring city of Epidaurus, which remained a firm ally of the Spartans. With unrest spreading through Lacedaemonia, the Spartans decided that it was time for a show of force. King Agis, the son of Archidamos, marched north with the full Spartan army and was duly met by the forces of the complete Democratic Alliance apart from the Athenians. (The Athenians were in something of a dilemma, having in different treaties undertaken to fight alongside both the alliance and the Spartans.)

As it turned out, on this occasion they were able to remain on the fence since both the alliance and the Spartan commanders backed down in the face of a major battle. This did not go down well at home for either side. The Spartans attacked their leaders for walking away when they had the chance to break the alliance, and the alliance bitterly castigated their leaders for missing their chance when they had the Spartans (as they saw it) at their mercy. Public opinion on both sides was committed to a trial of strength and hostilities became inevitable. After some dithering on the Athenian part, Alcibiades pushed his countrymen into abandoning the peace of Nicias and joining in on the alliance side. After a three-year pause Spartan and Athenian would again meet on the battlefield.

The confrontation happened at Mantinea in 418 BC. This was very much a traditional hoplite battle, and as such strongly favoured the Spartans who traditionally won any hoplite battles in which they were involved. In this case, the Mantineans took advantage of a temporary break in the Spartan line and pushed through. Despite being outmanoeuvred the Spartans won anyway, simply because they fought more stubbornly and ferociously than their opponents. The Athenians were protected by their cavalry and managed to extract their troops without major casualties, especially as the Spartans, as was their wont, did not follow up their victory by pursuing the routed enemy with any vigour.

The main Athenian casualty was the faction of Alcibiades, whom the fickle assembly now accused of leading the Athenians into an unnecessary and potentially catastrophic military adventure. It was typical of Alcibiades that his response to this setback was to rally the Athenians and lead them off to another unnecessary (and this time totally catastrophic) military adventure. This was the attempted Athenian conquest of Sicily. The Athenians decided that this large, rich and populous island would make a splendid addition to their empire. In addition, the resources of the island would tip the balance of power in mainland Greece irrevocably in their favour. After all, had not the Spartans done something similar when they became a leading power in Greece after their takeover of the larger, richer and more populous state of Messenia?

The Spartan response to this Athenian initiative was muted. The battle of Mantinea had comprehensively shredded the treaty with Athens yet the two states were not yet exactly at war. Nor, given the extent of Athenian power demonstrated by the expeditionary force to Sicily, did the Spartans particularly want to re-engage in active hostilities.

The proposed conquest of Sicily basically entailed the conquest of its principal city, Syracuse. The Athenians reckoned, possibly incorrectly, that once Syracuse had been subjugated then the rest of Sicily would fall into line. Therefore for the first year the expedition endeavoured to defeat Syracuse and to unite the rest of the island against that city. Both attempts failed. Though the Syracusans got the worst of the various clashes with the Athenians, the city held out. The remainder of the Sicilian cities showed little inclination to share the fate of Athenian 'allies' in the Delian League and declined Athenian offers of assistance with varying degrees of vehemence.

Syracuse was a Dorian foundation, and so the city's people looked to Sparta for help. Sparta was regarded as the leader of the Dorian people, but Syracuse was not a Spartan foundation. (The only city known to have been a Spartan colony was Tarentum on the Italian mainland opposite.) So where the Athenians had sent thousands of men and hundreds of ships to subdue Syracuse, the Spartans responded by sending one man – and he was not even a ranking Spartiate. His name was Gylippus, and he was of the *mothaces*, the second tier below Spartiate rank, although he, like others in his class, had also been through the brutal *agoge* which the Spartans reckoned to be the proper training of a young warrior. It is probable that Gylippus had fought both at Mantinea and in the war before that since he proved himself to be highly competent in military matters.

The point is that the Syracusans did not really need men or money from Sparta. The city had a substantial population and considerable financial resources, for the Greeks of Sicily were mostly more wealthy than their counterparts on the less fertile Greek mainland. What the Syracusans needed was advice from someone with experience in fighting the Athenians, and with the reputation and clout to knock the disorganized and amateurish Syracusan levies into shape. Gylippus provided all this and more. It is fair to say that his contribution turned the war around. The Syracusans had always had the potential for victory but it was Gylippus who properly galvanized the city to achieve it. His first step was to organize the building of a counter-wall to break any attempted Athenian encirclement, and then he established a blockade of the harbour where the Athenian fleet was positioned. The final result was the total destruction not only of the Athenian expedition but also of an equally large secondary force sent from Athens as reinforcements. Demosthenes, probably the most competent of the Athenian generals, was captured and killed in the debacle. So too was Nicias, whose refusal to accept the failure of the expedition which he commanded was largely responsible for its ultimate destruction.

Gylippus himself did not fare well in the aftermath of the siege. As was often the case with Spartans abroad, he seems to have become enamoured of the opportunities for easy money which his success had presented him. Booted out from Syracuse for financial malfeasance, it is unlikely that Gylippus returned home. The Spartan elite had been embarrassed at Mantinea where their poor leadership had been bailed out by the courage of the ordinary hoplites. They probably did not appreciate a second-rank *mothax* showing them how it should have been done. Wisely, Gylippus vanished and disappears from the history books, probably to live out his retirement on the Italian mainland with whatever he had retained of his ill-gotten gains.

Back to War

The failure of the Sicilian expedition had cost the Athenians a fortune in cash, a large part of their fleet and a huge part of their manpower. (The Syracusans kept their Athenian prisoners and worked them to death in the city's stone quarries.) Athens was vulnerable and the Spartans were goaded by their allies to take advantage of this. In principle, the Spartans were ready to resume the war. They owed the Athenians nothing, and the terms of the treaty of Nicias had been a dead letter since the battle of Mantinea. What the Spartans did not want to do was simply resume the war where they had left off. They had been losing then and without a new approach they were likely to keep losing now.

The best person to advise the Spartans about defeating the Athenians was currently a guest of the Spartan king. This was Alcibiades, now exiled from Athens on charges of mocking the gods. Since the Athenians regarded him as the author of the Sicilian debacle, Alcibiades had wisely decided not to go home to face charges. When the Athenians sentenced him to death *in absentia*, Alcibiades grimly remarked that he would show the Athenians he was still very much alive. This he did by providing the Spartans with sound advice. It was very clear that the key to breaking the Athenians was to break away the Athenian subject allies. To do that –

as the example of the unsuccessful revolt of Mytilene had shown in the previous war – the Spartans must first break the Athenian navy. This required a fleet.

However, the Spartans lacked both ships and a strong naval tradition. Therefore they needed money to buy ships and to pay mercenary rowers to crew them. The Spartans did not have much in the way of money but they knew someone who did: King Darius II of Persia. It seemed that the Persians were not only prepared to subsidise a renewed Spartan war effort, but were eager to do so. By some accounts it was Darius' subordinates Tissaphernes of Lydia and Pharnabazus of Phrygia who approached the Spartans with an offer to do just that. To further add to the Peloponnesian–Persian coalition, the Syracusans, not content with having hurled the Athenians off their island, were now eager to take the war to their would-be conquerors.

Whether because of Alcibiades' advice or through having pondered the matter on their own, the Spartans had decided that the problem with their previous seasonal raids on Attica was that they were just that: seasonal. The new plan involved not just going to Attica but staying there in a well fortified base that would choke off Athenian agriculture all year round. Furthermore, such a base would serve rather as Pylos served the Messenians. The base would welcome escaped slaves from the fields and the silver mines at Laurion (which mines, together with the annual tribute, made up most of Athens' annual income) and so cripple the Athenian economy.

This new war would be a very different affair. This time the Spartans had the man with a plan: Alcibiades. The former guiding lights of the Athenian war effort – Pericles, Kleon, Nicias and Demosthenes – had all fallen and Athens had only second-rate commanders to take their place. When hostilities resumed in 413, the Spartans proceeded with a purpose and direction which had hitherto been largely lacking.

Chapter 7

A Successful War and a Failed Peace

The Decelean War, 413–404 BC

Thanks to the Syracusans, the Peloponnesian–Persian alliance was able to put a fleet to sea almost immediately. Because of its earlier clash with the Athenians the Sicilian city already had a fleet to hand. Furthermore this fleet was crewed by veteran sailors with the rare experience of having fought the Athenians at sea, and having beaten them too.

At the same time as the Syracusan fleet arrived in the Aegean, Sparta's king Agis II advanced to Attica and set up a base in the village of Decelea, which he immediately set about converting into a formidable fortress. So strong an effect was this base to have on the permanent Spartan occupation of Attica that many historians have used it to distinguish this phase of the Peloponnesian War. Another name for the Decelean War is the Ionian War. While the previous round of combat had been fought mainly in northern Greece, this war was also fought on the seas and islands of the Aegean, and involved the cities of the coast of Asia Minor. The Greeks gave this region the overall name of Ionia.

The presence of a Peloponnesian fleet in Ionian waters had an immediate effect. The island of Chios renounced its membership of the Delian League; or to see it from an Athenian perspective, the island rebelled from the empire. When word of this revolt reached the people of Lesbos and Cyzicus both places sent ambassadors to the Spartans to enquire what help would be available should they too rebel against the Athenians. In response the Spartans decided to show what they could do for potential rebels by helping Chios.

A fleet was sent out, commanded by Alcibiades, who thus had the unique distinction of commanding troops on both sides during the war. For several very different reasons Alcibiades was seen as the right man for the job. Firstly, he knew the Athenian mindset and military tactics as only a former Athenian general could. Secondly, he went out of his way to show that he had been totally converted to the Spartan philosophy. He made every attempt to ingratiate himself with the Spartans:

The population watched spellbound as he adopted Spartan ways. He went about with his hair untrimmed, and tucked in with apparent enjoyment to their coarse bread and black porridge. It seemed incredible that this man who now plunged into cold baths had ever consulted a perfumer, employed a personal chef or worn [top-quality] Milesian wool. (Plutarch, *Alcibiades*, 23)

(The black porridge was a demonstration of how hard Alcibiades was trying. There is a story that a rare aristocratic visitor to Sparta was invited to dine in a Spartan mess and was fed this particular local delicacy. After a few spoonfuls of the porridge, the man was asked his opinion. He replied thoughtfully, 'I now understand why the Spartans do not fear death.')

One fan of the Spartan Alcibiades was Timaea, the wife of King Agis. Timaea had been deprived of male company for a while, because the last time she had had sex with her husband the pair had been interrupted by an earthquake. Agis took this as a sign of divine disapproval and had avoided the bed of his spouse ever since. That had been almost a year ago. So Agis was more than sceptical about the parentage of the bouncy baby boy whom his wife presented to him. It was not long for Alcibiades to be revealed as the father. He meant no disrespect, Alcibiades claimed, but wanted only to introduce his own blood into the royal line.

This was Sparta, so Agis did not have the usual recourse of an outraged husband in the ancient world. Spartan society encouraged women to take lovers if the result would be a healthy baby, although usually the husband expected to be consulted about the affair. The baby was certainly healthy so there was little that Agis could do. However, he was probably very unhappy about the entire affair. Overall, it seemed best for everybody if Alcibiades set off for Chios, where Agis might have hoped that the Athenians would do for the renegade what he legally could not.

The Athenians were overstretched, yet as ever they rallied with what the Spartans regarded as their unquenchable demonic energy. Despite the need to keep the rest of their restive empire under control with whatever remnants of their overstretched fleet had survived the Sicilian debacle, the Athenians still scraped together enough men and ships to promptly mount a siege of Chios and engage and defeat the Peloponnesians outside Miletus. In a rare display of opportunism the Spartans decided that since they were retreating in the direction of the island of Rhodes they may as well stop there and liberate the place, which they did.

The Battle for the Hellespont

While the war continued in the Aegean an equally furious contest was taking place on the diplomatic front. The Spartans and their allies had met with the Persian satrap Tissaphernes and were shocked to discover that the Persians expected an extremely high recompense. Basically, the reward for their help was to be the resumption of Persian control of all the cities of Asia Minor, and whatever members of the Delian League the Spartans might be able to pry away from the Athenians. On being flatly informed by the Spartans that this was not going to happen, Tissaphernes stormed out of the meeting and immediately opened negotiations with the Athenians.

As it happened the Athenians had a handy conduit for negotiations with Persia. The defeat outside Miletus had been sufficient cause for the Spartans to wonder if their commander Alcibiades had not been secretly assisting the Athenians. Whether or not he really believed this, Agis now had legal cause to sign Alcibiades' death warrant – probably with great satisfaction. Forewarned, Alcibiades fled to Tissaphernes and the pair set about scheming together. Obviously the Athenian assembly was strongly opposed to the return of Alcibiades. The people felt – with some justification – that Alcibiades was responsible for the death of their brothers and sons, and they still wanted to make him pay.

The aristocrats were more ambivalent. Keen to tap into the river of Persian money which had been flowing to Sparta, they were therefore ready to cautiously welcome the involvement of Alcibiades so long as he could help that happen. Alcibiades was happy to assist because he was again in need of allies and still nursed hopes of returning to his native city. Tissaphernes was ready to help but he had one condition which he passed on through Alcibiades: the Athenian democracy must go.

There was less opposition to this than might be expected. The Athenian aristocracy had never been really happy with the Athenian democracy, and would still prefer that they themselves remained in charge. Now Alcibiades and Tissaphernes dangled before the *demos* the prospect of bottomless Persian funds for their war against Sparta, if only they consented to return to oligarchic rule (and presumably abandoned their Ionian kinsmen, though this aspect was understandably downplayed). Consequently, in 411 BC an oligarchy took control of Athens. At first it was an extremely narrow oligarchy consisting of just 400 men but later the ruling class was expanded to include the top 5,000 men in the state.

Meanwhile, the Spartans might now be short of Persian funds but the Persians could not very well take back their fleet. Also, although Tissaphernes was inclining towards the Athenians, he was now working at cross-purposes with his rival Pharnabazus, satrap of north-western Anatolia, who still backed the Spartans. Accordingly, the Spartans moved their fleet north in order to benefit more fully from the support of their remaining Persian ally. There was also another reason for this move. During the Archidamian war the Spartans had observed that even as they destroyed Athenian crops in Attica, the enemy were importing grain by the shipload from the fields of their allies around the Black Sea.

Thanks to their base at Decelea the Spartans were still interdicting Athenian agricultural activity in Attica, but now their fleet gave them the chance to choke off overseas food supplies as well. Cities of the Hellespont were forewarned of Spartan intentions and immediately rebelled against Athens. As both Chalcedon and Byzantium became hostile, the strait connecting Athens to their resources in the Black Sea were now in the hands of Peloponnesian sympathizers. To make the Athenians even more miserable, at the same time the Spartans staged a landing in Euboea and captured the livestock which the people of Attica had evacuated to the island.

Given the magnitude of the threat now facing their state, it is unsurprising that the Athenians decided they needed all the help they could get and eagerly sought the support of the Persian enemy whom their empire had been formed to defeat. The new oligarchy immediately set about proving its worth and engaged the Spartans at sea. The Peloponnesians might now match the Athenians in ships but apart from the Syracusan contingent they were still inferior in seamanship. A Spartan admiral called Mindarus lost a good part of Sparta's new fleet when he was defeated at Cynossema in the Thracian Chersonese.

A further series of defeats followed and the Athenians retrieved the rebel city of Cyzicus. A further naval action at the Hellespont – which saw Alcibiades yet again in command of Athenian ships – conclusively broke the Spartan stranglehold on Athenian grain supplies. It also convinced those Athenian allies contemplating rebellion that the Athenian navy was still capable of enforcing the city's will. The rash of rebellions largely came to an end.

This series of victories seems to have restored Athenian self-confidence and the democracy was restored. For the Spartans it seemed as though matters were returning to the stalemate of the Archidamian war, where the Spartan superiority in land battles was negated by their inability to control the sea. As they had done two decades previously the Spartans offered peace terms, this time on the basis that both sides would keep what they had gained.

Athenian scepticism regarding this offer was understandable. The Spartans held Euboea and had strong garrisons in the Bosporus. Should peace break out, the Spartans would be free from interference from the Athenian navy. They could strengthen their positions to the point where they would be able to choke off the Athenian grain supply the moment war broke out anew. The breaking of the Spartan promise to return Amphipolis after the previous round of combat added to Athenian distrust of Spartan good faith.

The Final Phase: 409–404 BC

At this point the landlubberly Spartans produced their version of a black swan: a Spartiate who was also a great admiral. This was Lysander, a man who had grown up in poverty but was of noble lineage – his family claimed direct descent from Hercules. Despite his lowly upbringing Lysander possessed considerable diplomatic ability and he befriended Agesilaus, the brother of Agis. (One tradition claims the pair were lovers.) Lysander leveraged his influence with Agesilaus into command of a Spartan fleet, and from there he moved to the coast of Asia Minor.

The feud between Pharnabazus and Tissaphernes over which side to support in the war had gone to the royal court for arbitration. The Persian monarchy's long-standing dislike of the Athenians had brought King Darius over to the Spartan side – and the Athenian return to democracy certainly did not help Tissaphernes' case. Tissaphernes was superseded by a superior – a royal prince known today as Cyrus the Younger. He was already inclined to the Peloponnesian side and found Lysander a convivial ally, especially as the Spartans had now abandoned their principled stand to defend the Ionian cities. Cyrus and Lysander agreed between them that once Athens had been beaten, the cities of Ionia were to fall once more under Persian sovereignty.

Sparta was now prepared to countenance this previously unthinkable volt-face because Persian help was urgently needed. The Athenians had come storming back into the war. In 409 they recaptured several Ionian cities and were clearly in command of the sea. In fact, things were going so well that Alcibiades dared to make a return to Athens in the hope that he had been forgiven. As it turned out, he had not. As soon as Athens suffered a naval defeat at Notion in 406 the people turned on him. There was some justice in this, as the defeated admiral had obtained his command thanks to the patronage of Alcibiades. However, the idea that this appointee was a total incompetent does little credit to the skill with which Lysander commanded the Peloponnesian fleet.

The prestige that Lysander gained from his victory inspired other Spartan leaders who wanted a share of the glory of naval triumphs.

Lysander was promptly displaced by the better-connected Callicrates. Sadly, Callicrates' political skill was somewhat greater than his ability as an admiral. He attempted to blockade the Athenian fleet at Mytilene, but was defeated at Arginusae by an Athenian relief force. Callicrates went down with his fleet.

Arginusae was to be the last Athenian naval victory. Decades of war had drained the Athenian reserves. The Spartan fortress at Decelea not only prevented the Athenians from working the silver mines that were a major source of their revenue, but also gave sanctuary to the thousands of slaves who fled the mines to take refuge there. The Athenian empire, once a source of pride and revenue, was now a money pit into which Athenian funds were constantly poured. This was because the desperately over-extended Athenian fleet was consuming more money trying to keep the restive allies under control than the allies paid in their annual contributions. With the Spartans now a constant presence in Aegean waters, the Athenians could not extort any more gold from their subjects without inspiring further expensive rebellions.

The Spartans had no such problems, awash as they were with Persian funds. They speedily replaced their naval losses and decided that maybe it would be best if Lysander commanded their fleet once again. However, the Spartan constitution did not permit a man to twice hold the position of *navarchos* (admiral). Therefore Lysander took to the water officially as the deputy to a sock-puppet official commander, although in reality he had complete control. Persian enthusiasm had waned when Callicrates took the helm but once Lysander was back in command Cyrus' support was unconditional.

Meanwhile, the admirals who had won the Athenian victory at Arginusae had been condemned by the city's fickle assembly. Immediately after the battle, the admirals had decided that the remaining Athenian ships were too precious to risk in an approaching storm and ran for shelter without stopping to save those survivors of damaged ships who were still in the water. When the admirals returned to Athens they found a less-than-grateful people waiting for them. The furious relatives of the drowned had whipped up a mob which duly found the admirals guilty of abandoning the shipwrecked men to their fate. In a travesty of a trial the assembly voted for the death penalty. It was not democracy's proudest moment.

Even the principled resistance of one man, Socrates, was not enough to prevent a legalized lynching. As a result of the condemnation, those admirals whom the Athenians could get their hands on were executed while the remainder fled into exile. This meant that the most capable naval commanders Athens possessed were lost to the fleet, which was in any case under-strength as the near-bankrupt city was unable to send supplies or reinforcements to those ships which had survived the battle.

Thanks to Lysander and the Persians the Spartans had everything the Athenians lacked: supplies, reinforcements and a competent commander. Lysander won a resounding victory at Aegispotomai in September 405, a battle in which the last Athenian ships were destroyed. Without a fleet Athens was defenceless so this Spartan victory made the ultimate defeat of Athens inevitable. Soon after Aegispotomai Athens itself came under siege, this time by both land and sea. The long war was effectively won.

In 404 BC the population of Athens was starving and there was no prospect of relief in sight. The people accepted that their position was hopeless and the city surrendered. After nearly sixty years of intermittent warfare, it seemed as though Sparta had finally attained its objective. Athens was humbled and Sparta reigned supreme.

The Spartan Hegemony

It took a while for Greece to comprehend that the long war was finally over. The long-drawn-out Peloponnesian War was all that most Greeks had known all their lives. Now the war had reached its end, the Hellenes had to come to terms with the problems of peace. Of these problems, the first and most urgent was – what was to be done with Athens?

By the end of the war the Athenians had few friends. Even those allies who had started the war favourable to the city had been offended by the ever-increasing demands for tribute. They were also alienated by the fact that they were fighting the Spartans, not the Persians, which had been the original intention of the alliance. Sparta's allies were out for blood. The Thebans, and to a lesser degree the Corinthians, had a very clear idea of how to proceed against the defeated city. Athens should share the fate of Plataea. Its walls should be torn down, its buildings demolished and the people sold into slavery.

Lysander was inclined to agree, for he had proven a rough conqueror. A poet joked that tavern-keepers were accustomed to giving patrons a first cupful of sweet wine before diluting it with harsh vinegar. Lysander was worse, the poet claimed, because he allowed not even a taste of sweet freedom to the Greek cities released from the Athenian empire. Instead he immediately imposed upon them rule by a *harmost* (the Spartan word for a military governor) in conjunction with a ten-man council composed of men Lysander thought most likely to be loyal to himself.

In the way of Greek cities of the era, once given unfettered control these ten men immediately set about killing or driving into exile enemies real or imagined. Cities that had suffered only financial hardship during the war suddenly found their leading civic figures rounded up and executed, with the active support of the Spartan occupiers. The revenues the cities had once paid to Athens were now diverted to Lysander.

Fortunately for the Athenians, the fact that Lysander had set up what was virtually a private empire in the Aegean had not gone unnoticed in Sparta. To Lysander's great credit, he was honest enough to immediately start transferring to the Spartan state the immense fortune that he had gathered. Nevertheless the question on the minds of the Ephors was – would Lysander be as ready to hand over political control?

The first step in reasserting the authority of Sparta's leaders came in the form of a terse decree from the Ephors. This ordered the Athenians to tear down their city walls, but otherwise left matters to Lysander and the others on the spot. However, the decree stated that if the Athenians tore down their walls 'there would be peace' – an explicit statement that Athens was not to be destroyed. The Athenian diplomat who had helped to arrange these terms attempted to appease the Athenians by pointing out that if a lack of city walls meant that a city was in dire straits, then Sparta was in even worse shape than Athens.

Demolishing the walls was about the best the Spartans could do with Athens because of the nature of war and politics in ancient Greece. The Long Walls connecting Athens to Piraeus were demolished, but what happened to the other walls is less certain. Archaeology shows that at least some were left standing. Simply flattening Athens and killing or enslaving the population would not work, because the city occupied prime land and sooner rather than later someone would reoccupy the site.

Furthermore, removing Athens as a counter-balance to Thebes was a bad idea because Thebes was proving to be a problem already. Unless they wanted Boeotia to be as powerful as Sparta, having the Thebans expand into Attica (and they would) was not recommended. The Spartans could not occupy the site themselves because they hardly had enough Spartans to occupy Laconia and were stretched to capacity by holding down Messenia as well.

So the best the Spartans could do was to make Athens compliant by removing those walls which enabled it to withstand a Spartan siege, and then imposing an oligarchic government loyal to Sparta. The Spartan authorities probably knew that this was a short-term fix but, as we have just discussed, there were no satisfactory long-term solutions.

Accordingly, on a set day, teams of workmen assembled and began to pull down the walls of Athens. This was accompanied by a merry bonfire which consumed whatever remained of the Athenian fleet (although Lysander allowed the city to keep twelve ships). To the sound of music played by specially imported flute girls, delegations from Sparta's allies relaxed with garlands on their heads and watched the spectacle.

It seemed to be a demonstration of Sparta's triumph yet in truth Sparta had been gravely injured during the long war. As we have seen, the fundamental problem remained: Sparta had a demographic deficit of Spartiates. The casualties inflicted during the war had hastened the downward spiral in numbers, as we can assume that the widows of the fallen inherited their estates and added them to those of their next husbands – men who may well have also died in the war. According to Aristotle, writing a generation later, in his day women owned almost half the land in Sparta. While this was no bad thing in itself, it meant that the number of Spartiates maintained by their own estates was still dropping. This trend had already been established by the end of the Peloponnesian War and it remained as a canker eating away at the foundation of the Spartan state for over a century.

Furthermore, at the end of the Persian Wars Sparta had been admired, feared and respected. At the end of the Peloponnesian War Sparta was widely disliked for its overbearing ways, despised for having taken Persian money in exchange for the freedom of the Greeks of Ionia, and less feared than previously. Although ultimately defeated, the Athenians had shown that the Spartans definitely could be beaten.

In previous centuries it was a Spartan tradition not to make war on one state repeatedly, lest that state become accomplished in warfare through constant practice. By the end of the Peloponnesian War everyone had been practising a great deal. All Greek states now had a solid contingent of veteran warriors. These men were certainly not impressed by Spartan pretensions to innate military superiority, and the leaders of Sparta's former allies were quite prepared to resist any attempts by Sparta's leaders to throw their weight around.

But now Sparta had a cash flow problem. With their leftover Persian money, plus the revenues of the former Athenian empire diverted to their state, the Spartans had all too much money flowing in. Despite their reputation for despising filthy lucre it turned out that rather a lot of Spartans wanted to get their hands on it. The Ephors responded by making the possession of bullion illegal for private individuals, and insisted that cash could only be handled by the state. 'As though that which was publicly honoured could be privately despised,' remarks Plutarch scornfully. 'Public malpractice taints private life much faster than individuals can corrupt entire cities.' (Plutarch, *Lysander*, 17)

Apart from the problem of having too much cash on hand, the Spartan kings also had to work out what to do with Lysander, who was actually mightier than they. Fortunately Lysander seemed to be working hard to accomplish his own downfall. He held the Aegean cities in the palm of his hand and was proving something of a bloodthirsty tyrant. His favourite saying, 'Cheat children at dice and men with false promises', quickly meant that soon nobody trusted a word that he said, especially as those who stood in his way were lured into his power by false assurances of safety and then executed. Eventually the Persian satrap Pharnabazus wrote to the Spartan kings. He complained that if Lysander continued to behave in this way, there was going to be a general rebellion. Alarmed, the Spartan authorities recalled their wayward general.

Lysander came home bearing with him a letter which he had persuaded Pharnabazus to write. This letter was believed by Lysander to contain a refutation of all the previous charges, but unknown to him the wily Persian satrap had at the last moment replaced the letter and given Lysander a different one to take to Sparta. The letter was identical in appearance to the one Pharnabazus had written for Lysander but very different in content. This led to the bewildered Spartan assembly of elders (the *gerousia*) trying to understand why Lysander had handed over with such confident aplomb a letter which, once the seals were broken and the contents read, contained a scathing and detailed denunciation of the man and all his works.

Faced with the hostility of the kings and Ephors, Lysander was prevented from returning to Asia while the Spartan authorities began the slow task of transferring the loyalty of Aegean cities from Lysander the Spartan to Sparta itself. It did not help that the Spartan kingship itself now had a credibility problem.

King Agis had wanted to bring to heel Elis in the north-west Peloponnese and did so after a successful campaign against that state. Thereafter he had proceeded to Delphi to give thanks for his victory – but died on the journey. This left the issue of who should succeed to the Eurypontid line of kings. In the usual course of events the throne would pass uneventfully to the king's son – in this case a young man called Leotychides. The problem, as we saw earlier, was that there was a very good case for arguing that Leotychides was not the son of Agis, but rather was the illegitimate son of the renegade Alcibiades. (Alcibiades was now exiled from both

Athens and Sparta and was living out his days in Thrace. There he was eventually assassinated, although by whom is uncertain. By that time the list of people wanting him dead included almost everybody in the known world.)

Apart from Leotychides, the other candidate for the Eurypontid kingship was Agesilaus, the brother of the late Agis. The opponents of Agesilaus could also make a good case against him. For a start, Agesilaus was 'lame'. Given his later career it is highly unlikely that his lameness was serious, but to the Spartans any physical defect was disturbing. Indeed, if Agesilaus had not been royalty, and therefore exempt from the strictures facing normal Spartiates, he might well not have survived to an age where he could be considered for the succession. When consulted about who should be king the Oracle at Delphi appeared to weigh in against Agesilaus:

> Sparta – you are now so very proud.
> But think of this.
> If from you, so sure-footed,
> There arises a maimed king
> Then you will be crushed by misfortune
> And the blows of man-destroying war.

Pretty clear, one might think, especially as Leotychides had managed to prevail on Agis while the old king was on his deathbed, and had been recognized as the royal heir. At this point Lysander joined the debate on the side of his partner. He managed to convince the people that the 'maimed king' would be Leotychides, since allegations of his bastardy would for ever undermine his credibility. Lysander still had considerable influence in the state and his argument carried the day. Agesilaus was duly selected.

The Persian Wars, Reloaded

It would be wrong to assume that Sparta now went to war with Persia purely because Lysander had a bone to pick with the satrap Pharnabazus. After the discreditable deal by which the Spartans had taken Persian silver in exchange for the freedom of Ionia, Sparta had considerably tarnished its reputation as the leader of the Hellenes. The Spartans were eager to once more burnish their image and fighting Persia was a good way to do this.

Nor were the Persians very happy with Sparta's leadership of Greece. Directly after the Peloponnesian War Cyrus the Younger had recruited many disbanded Greek warriors from both sides. He had used this mercenary army in an attempt to overthrow his brother, who had become the Persian king after the death of Darius II. Cyrus might well have succeeded in his bid for power had he not perished while mismanaging the climactic battle of Cunaxa in 401 BC. The death of Cyrus left 10,000 Greek mercenaries stuck in the middle of Parthia. Their *de facto* commander was the Athenian soldier Xenophon, who later wrote the *Anabasis* ('*The Journey Back*'), a stirring tale of how the 10,000 made their way home after a march of around a thousand miles through hostile territory.

The Persian army was not far behind this retreating army, not least because the Greek cities under Persian control had supported Cyrus in his rebellion. With Cyrus' death the Greek cities were in a state of precarious independence which the Persians were determined to crush. The Ionians appealed to Sparta as the leading military power in Greece, and the Spartans leapt at the chance to regain the mantle of the protectors of the Hellenes. Within a short time an army of Spartans and their allies had arrived in Asia Minor, led by Agesilaus – although since Lysander was at the king's right hand, many were uncertain who was in charge.

In fact, the troubles had begun even before Agesilaus left Europe. For a start, while minor cities of the Peloponnesian League had contributed men to the coming campaign, Thebes, Athens and Corinth had pointedly refused to collaborate. A further diplomatic spat had followed. Agesilaus was at the port of Aulis in Boeotia, in central Greece, where he was preparing to make a sacrifice for a safe crossing to Asia Minor. This ceremony was rudely interrupted by the Theban authorities who intervened to prevent the king's sacrifice from going ahead. They insisted that a sacrifice on Boeotian soil should only be performed by one of their own priests. That the Boeotians were prepared to interrupt a Spartan king in the middle of a religious rite was an example of the new assertiveness that Sparta's allies had recently been demonstrating. This ill-omened incident probably made Agesilaus even less prepared to tolerate unwanted assertiveness in his own subjects – including and principally Lysander.

The people of Asia Minor might not have liked Lysander's earlier rule, but they had become accustomed to it. When they heard that Lysander was back the people of Asia Minor hastened either to renew diplomatic ties or to excuse their previous complaints against him. The actual ruler, Agesilaus, was more than irritated as a flood of delegates and embassies passed him by in their rush to ingratiate themselves with Lysander.

The clash of these two powerful personalities was resolved by the fact that only one of them had real authority, and that was Agesilaus. The only official rank that the king permitted Lysander was 'carver of the royal meats'. All petitions directed through Lysander received such short shrift from the king that Lysander was eventually forced to suggest that petitioners address their requests elsewhere. Finally, an embittered Lysander returned to Sparta leaving Agesilaus to prosecute the war under his sole authority.

Sparta was helped by the fact that Egypt was (again) in revolt against its Persian masters and this led to a diffusion of the Persian military effort. As a result Agesilaus was able to liberate (or conquer) a number of cities and amass a considerable reserve of booty. What he was not able to do was advance far inland, because the Persian cavalry was far superior to his own. The Persian horsemen could not face hoplites in open battle, but they could interdict the Spartan supply lines unless the army remained close enough to the coast to be resupplied by sea.

The reliance of the Persians on their cavalry was clearly demonstrated when Agesilaus decided that he had mustered enough cavalry from his allies to advance on Persia's regional capital, Sardis. The Persian cavalry immediately cut off any outlying foragers and advance troops that Agesilaus sent out, and forced the king to deploy his men so that they marched in a hollow square with their baggage in the centre.

The years of campaigning against the unconventional Athenians had taught the Spartans a trick or two. As Agesilaus neared Sardis he abruptly reversed course. The Persians assumed the Spartans were retreating and promptly began to harass the Spartan rearguard. Yet when Agesilaus began his retreat he had not taken his whole army with him: an elite corps of men was hidden in a nearby wood. When the Spartan army and the Persian pursuit had moved past the wood, the Spartans concealed therein charged out, trapping the Persian cavalry between themselves and the rearguard. The result was a Spartan victory, although how decisive this victory was depends on whether one follows the historian Diodorus Siculus, who puts the Persian death toll at 6,000 (Book 14.80), or the usually more reliable Oxyrhynchus historian, who estimates Persian casualties at literally a tenth of that figure (*Oxyrhynchus*, 12–13).

We get yet another account from the historian Xenophon. According to him, the Persian cavalrymen were caught not between two infantry forces but between the Spartan infantry and a river. In any case the result was the same: the Persian king lost confidence in the ability – and perhaps the will – of Tissaphernes to prosecute the war, and the satrap was replaced and beheaded. Tissaphernes' replacement came with the authority to negotiate. Agesilaus agreed that he would cease his advance inland in exchange for the autonomy of the Greek cities in the satrapy – and a large sum of cash. Then with peace secured on that front, the Spartan king moved north to attack Pharnabazus.

Unable to offer much by way of resistance, Pharnabazus was eventually forced to fall back on moral suasion. He arranged a meeting with Agesilaus:

> Agesilaus and his entourage were first to arrive for the meeting, and he threw himself down to wait in a shady place with lush grass. When Pharnabazus arrived he was ashamed to see Agesilaus thus, for he himself had brought embroidered rugs and soft cushions to recline upon. Therefore with no further ado, he joined Agesilaus on the grass regardless of the damage to his wonderful clothes with their delicate fabric and subtle dyes. (Plutarch, *Agesilaus*, 12)

Pharnabazus made the justified complaint that he was receiving harsh recompense for all the help that he had given the Spartans against Athens. Agesilaus agreed that this was unjust but averred that he was making war on Persia not against Pharnabazus personally. If Pharnabazus would change sides, or even remain neutral, the Spartans would happily renew their alliance. Reluctantly the Persian acknowledged the Spartan point, and the two men parted personal friends yet perforce still also enemies.

Exactly what Agesilaus intended to achieve in his eastern adventures is uncertain. His original mission had been to keep the Persian armies from retaking the rebel Greek cities of Ionia, but once that objective had been achieved the Spartan king showed little inclination to return home. Instead he concentrated on training the citizen levies of the newly liberated Greek cities. This may have been simply to better enable those cities to resist later attempts by the Persians to reassert their dominion. It might also, as historians both contemporary and modern have speculated, indicate that Agesilaus was raising and augmenting troops for a much more ambitious project: the conquest of the Persian empire (or at least, given the immense size of that empire, the conquest of Asia Minor and parts of the Levant).

Realizing the threat, the Persians fought back in the manner they had found to be most effective. Large sums of Persian silver began to find their way into the treasuries of anti-Spartan aristocrats in Thebes, Argos and Corinth. Even the Athenians, although Xenophon denies that they took 'bribes', were happy to accept 'subsidies' to help with the back-pay of their army and the fleet which – to intense Spartan irritation – had grown far larger than the permitted twelve ships. In fact the current Athenian leader, a man called Conan, was actually invited to an audience with the Persian king.

The upshot of all this intense Persian behind-the-scenes activity was that Thebes began to adopt a more independent stance and the Thebans encouraged the Athenians to do the same. Thanks partly to Persian money and partly to poor Spartan diplomacy and man-management, the Spartan hegemony in central Greece was rapidly crumbling away. It was only a matter of time before the Persian king attained his objective and forced Agesilaus and his men to return to deal with the deteriorating situation on the Greek mainland. The conquest of Persia would have to be left to another king, and at a future date.

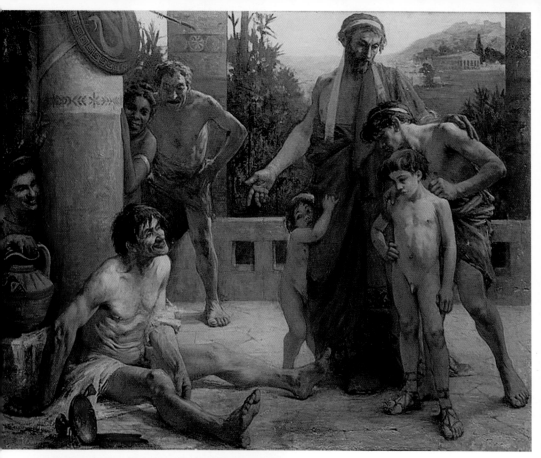

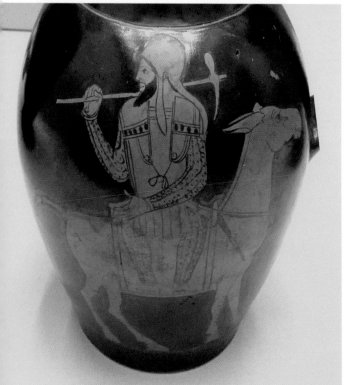

A Spartan points out a drunken slave to his sons; painting by Fernand Sabatte, 1900. The Spartans used to deliberately get helots drunk to show their children the effects of losing self-control.

A Persian combat engineer mounted on a donkey. Note the Greek-style linothorax, the result of constant cultural and military interaction between the Greek and Persian civilizations.
(*P. Matyszak*)

(*Left*) The entrance to the Temple of Apollo at Delphi. The Delphic oracle was politically important to the religiously scrupulous Spartans, and Apollo, the God who supplied the oracles, was correspondingly revered. (*Jeremy Day*)

(*Right*) Persian archer, from an Athenian black-figure vase. Persian bowmen were brave, but unable to cope with the Greek tactic of closing quickly with heavily armoured hoplites. (*P. Matyszak*)

Greek infantry. This frieze on the Elgin marbles shows the evolution of the Greek helmet from the head-encompassing Corinthian style to lighter gear which protected only the top of the skull. (*P. Matyszak*)

The Leonidian in modern Sparta. This was somewhere between a monument and a shrine, built to honour not only the king, but the ideals of bravery and self-sacrifice which he represented. *(Jackie Whalen)*

View across Sparta to Mt Parnon. Mt Parnon was visible from the acropoli of both Athens and Sparta – a further reminder of how small an area classical Greece encompassed. *(Jackie Whalen)*

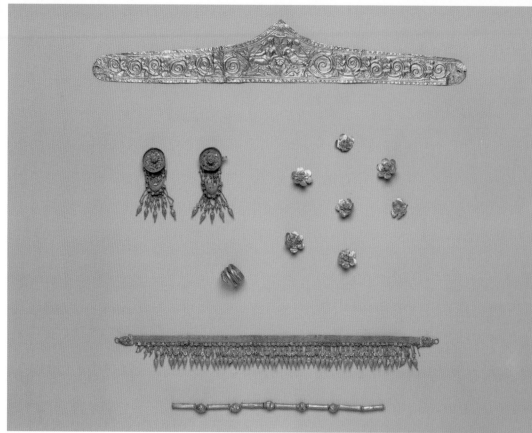

Contemporary woman's jewellery – in the later years aristocratic Spartan women developed a taste for such decorations which was far from the city's austere image. (*Metropolitan Museum of Art, New York*)

A mother arms her son before battle. Even in relatively enlightened Sparta, women were under-valued. However, they appear to have fully subscribed to Spartan values, and tales abound of mothers urging their sons to be heroic and/or die in the attempt. (*P. Matyszak*)

Mount Ithome depicted in an 1882 woodcut, looking much as it would have done to besieging Spartans 2,000 years previously.

The medieval monastery at Mystras – Mystras being the more secure location to which the population of Sparta moved after the fall of Rome made the original city location of Sparta too dangerous to defend. (*M. Bretherton*)

(*Left*) King Nabis, portrait taken from a contemporary coin. It was typical of the Spartans that they adopted coinage much later than the rest of Greece, and – as with other 'modern' concepts – they rather bungled the implementation.

(*Right*) Head of Philip II of Macedon. The rise of nation-states such as Rome and Macedon meant that the traditional Greek *polis* was outmatched in manpower and resources. Sparta was not the only *polis* which failed to compete.

A view of the Spartan acropolis looking west across modern Sparta. (*Jackie Whalen*)

Modern Sparta with the Taygetos range in the background. (*Jackie Whalen*)

The remains of the theatre, as seen from the Spartan acropolis. Despite their puritannical image, the Spartans valued highly both song and dance. (*Jackie Whalen*)

The remains of the walls of Sparta. For generations it was the proud boast of the Spartans that their walls were the shields of their warriors. However, the declining Spartiate population eventually rendered that boast unfeasible. (*M. Bretherton*)

This single olive tree of tough wood shows the difficulty involved in destroying even the few acres of olive trees shown on the right. (*Tomas Jokl*)

Chapter 8

The Lame King

'Oh, the barbarous ill deeds devised by the Greeks!' Here Plutarch quotes Euripides, lamenting the 'jealousy which now formed the Greeks into battle array against one another ... and turned again upon themselves those weapons directed at the Barbarians [Persians]'.

Back in Sparta Lysander had allegedly been intriguing to have Agesilaus replaced as king. The replacement Lysander had in mind for the absent monarch was none other than himself. According to reports which circulated after his death, Lysander was making arrangements for a series of 'secret' oracular pronouncements which were to be discovered by a young man who was allegedly a son of Apollo. Once revealed, these oracles would announce a terrible fate for Sparta if the city did not abandon its hereditary kingship and replace it with the rule of whomever in the state was 'most suitable'. This laudably egalitarian plan was based on the fact that Lysander had already determined that the most suitable person to rule Sparta was himself. He now set about attempting to persuade the rest of Sparta to fall in with his plan.

In keeping with a long and discreditable tradition among Spartan leaders, Lysander first tried to persuade the supposedly impartial Delphic priestess to produce an oracle in his favour. However, his efforts at persuasion were so heavy-handed that all he got in return was a complaint to the Ephors about his conduct. With the endorsement of the gods withheld thanks to the obduracy of the Oracle, Lysander could not yet reveal the prophecy demanding that the kingship be awarded to the most suitable person because he first needed to prove beyond doubt that he *was* that person.

There was of course a more straightforward way of becoming renowned in a warrior state – to be a renowned warrior. Lysander now addressed himself to increasing his already considerable fame in that regard. The first thing a would-be warrior needs is a war. Sparta was currently at peace, apart from the war with Persia from which Lysander had been firmly excluded. Fortunately, the situation in Greece was such that Sparta had a wide range of potential enemies whom a man of ill-will and political influence could provoke into war. Lysander chose Thebes.

There can be no doubt that Thebes and Sparta each had a long and growing list of grievances with the other. The Thebans complained that the Spartans were interfering in a war they were fighting in nearby Phocis, and they also alleged that the Spartans were meddling in their internal political affairs. The Thebans had been alone among the allies in complaining that, as fellow belligerents in the war against Athens, they were entitled a tenth share of the spoils of that war – spoils which the Spartans kept tightly to themselves.

In their turn the Spartans were incensed by the role that Thebes had played in restoring the Athenian democracy. The Spartans had set up in Athens an oligarchic government known to later historians as the Thirty Tyrants. Tyrannical the Thirty certainly were and, following the example of their erstwhile patron Lysander, these men attempted to rule through terror. The Spartans abetted them in this by passing a decree that anyone who fled the rule of the Thirty in Athens should be returned to that city for punishment. Anyone who sheltered such refugees would be considered an enemy of Sparta.

Having recently been keen advocates of the total destruction of Athens, the Thebans now decided to spite Sparta by becoming the protectors of Athens and its democracy. They passed a decree of their own declaring that every house in Boeotia should be open to Athenian refugees. Anyone who failed to help them would be subject to a swingeing fine. Furthermore, if anyone was moving through Boeotia with weapons or men intended for use against the Athenian tyranny, the people of Boeotia were instructed to look the other way.

Theban support was thus key to the democratic revolution in Athens. A man called Thrasybulus gathered armed supporters in Boeotia and took them to Athens, where the Tyrants were duly overthrown and their leader, a man called Critias, was killed. Democratic Athens immediately formed an alliance with Thebes and, as we have seen, opened diplomatic relations with the Persian king.

In short, Sparta certainly had a bone to pick with its recalcitrant Theban ally, but this did not mean that Sparta had to go to war about it. There was nothing in the quarrel with Thebes that could not have been resolved by patient diplomacy. Moreover, the Spartans could have accepted that the democratic revolution in Athens had much less to do with anti-Spartan sentiment than with disgust at the methods and maladministration of the Thirty. Had they done so, there was no reason why an amicable peace could not have been reached with both Athens and Thebes. After all, the new Athenian government was striving hard for peace and reconciliation.

Therefore peace was certainly achievable but for two powerful factors working against it. One of these was the money that the Persians were persuasively pumping into the pockets of warmongers everywhere. The second factor was Lysander, who needed a war for his own political purposes.

Matters favoured the warmongers. Lysander's faction was able to persuade the Ephors and the assembly that Thebes needed to be brought forcibly to heel – and given recent Theban conduct, one doubts that much persuasion was needed. On the other side the Thebans reckoned that they had taken all the Spartan bullying that they were going to take. With Athens, Argos and Corinth on their side, and with Persia openly backing their cause, the Thebans planned on giving the Spartans a run for their money. Both sides felt the same way: that is, that they had a good chance of winning if they went to war against an over-mighty city which had become a bit too presumptuous. Under those circumstances peace stood little chance.

The Corinthian War, 395–387 BC

This war is so called because most of the fighting on land happened near Corinth. As the leading cities in the Peloponnese, Corinth, Argos and Sparta had an unhealthy three-way relationship. Sparta and Argos were in the closest proximity and the two cities loathed each other. Therefore Spartan policy generally aimed at retaining Corinth on Sparta's side and so keeping Argos subdued. However, Sparta's indifference to allied sensibilities during and after the Peloponnesian War had alienated Corinth, which had promptly fallen into the welcoming arms of Argos.

Therefore, the main Spartan objective in going to war was to give Thebes a good kicking and in the process restore oligarchic rule in Athens. A close second on the Spartan list of priorities was prising apart the alliance of Corinth and Argos. On the other side the main intention of the alliance arrayed against Sparta was simply to survive. This would prove – to themselves, to the rest of Greece and above all to Sparta itself – that the Spartans were nowhere near as powerful as they thought they were and that threats and military power alone were insufficient to make Sparta the arbiter of Greek affairs.

The Spartans opened hostilities by advancing in two columns upon the Boeotian city of Haliartus, a small but strategic city some 100 kilometres from Athens. One column was led by Pausanias, the Agaid Spartan king, the other, in the absence of Agesilaus, who was still in Asia Minor, was led by Lysander. So far, from Lysander's point of view all was going to plan.

His plan may well have been intended to remove from power not only Agesilaus but also Pausanias. The Agaid king was a known moderate and a conservative who disliked military adventures. There is no doubt that Pausanias would have been violently opposed to Lysander as a fellow monarch. Therefore if the hereditary kingship were to be overturned and Lysander became king, then Pausanias would have to go as well.

Much of this is speculation, because by definition plots tend to be secretive. However, this speculation makes sense of what would otherwise be an oddly uncharacteristic move by Lysander. In the war against Athens Lysander had shown himself to be an almost obsessively cautious commander who would not strike until he had manipulated the odds overwhelmingly into his favour. Even though he probably had enough support among the Spartan aristocracy to make a bid for power, Lysander wanted to make completely sure that he would succeed before he made any overt move.

Yet now, immediately after he had turned the small (but strategically located) Boeotian town of Orchomenus against Thebes, the usually cautious Lysander immediately advanced on Haliartus without waiting for Pausanias. This was rash enough, but once he reached the city Lysander took a yet greater risk by moving his men dangerously close to the walls. The Thebans saw that the Spartans were poorly positioned and attacked, causing substantial Spartan casualties. For this setback the blame fell on Pausanias, whom Lysander's supporters accused of having arrived too late to support Lysander in his attack on Haliartus. Pausanias was put on trial for his tardiness. Facing the death penalty if convicted, Pausanias decided not to take his chances with the court. He fled to exile in Tegea.

If forcing Pausanias into exile had been Lysander's master plan all along, then this was the reason why the usually cautious general had behaved with such irrational daring. What looked like a minor Spartan defeat was actually a highly complex operation which had been brought to a successful conclusion. In theory, with Pausanias gone, Lysander would now be in sole command.

However, the problem with such operations is that the more complex they are the more there is to go wrong. In this case, by moving his unsupported army too close to Haliartus, Lysander had put not only his troops but himself in danger. The army by and large survived. Lysander did not. He perished beneath the walls of Haliartus and certain knowledge of exactly what he was trying to do in his foolhardy attack died with him.

Apart from removing both Lysander and Pausanias from the war the engagement at Haliartus had two other significant consequences. Firstly, the *ad hoc* alliance between Thebes, Athens and the Argive–Corinthian coalition was formalized by treaty, and secondly, Sparta had now lost in quick succession King Agis, Lysander and King Pausanias. Since the son of Pausanias was too young for a field command, Sparta was desperately short of leaders. It was at this point that Agesilaus was urgently recalled from his war in Persia.

The imminent return of Agesilaus and his army forced the allies into action. Agesilaus was returning overland by way of Thrace and Thessaly, more or less along the route taken by invading Persian armies of nearly a hundred years before. Another Spartan army, this one commanded by a regent in place of the under-age king, advanced north out of the Peloponnese to join up with Agesilaus. If they were not to be caught between the two Spartan armies the allies had to attack one or the other. Since the army coming down from the north consisted of veteran soldiers under an experienced commander, the allies decided to first try their luck against the relatively inexperienced troops coming up from the south under an untried leader.

The battle was fought at Nemea, not far from Corinth and very close to where in legend Hercules had fought a more personal battle with an invincible lion. The actual combat was a typical hoplite slugging match of the type at which the Spartans excelled. The Spartans were in the place of honour in a Greek battle line, which was the right. Since their enemies followed the same convention the result of the battle was not unexpected. The Spartans broke the weaker troops in front of them (in this case the Athenians), while the inferior forces of their Peloponnesian allies were broken by the top soldiers in the Theban alliance. In the end Spartan discipline made the difference. Having overwhelmed the Athenians, the Spartans then turned and beat the Argives, then the Corinthians and finally the Thebans as each army returned exhausted from its pursuit of the beaten Peloponnesians.

It was a resounding Spartan victory. It was also – apart from the considerable propaganda value – a pointless one. Because the action had taken place south of Corinth, there was still no way of getting past that city's command of the isthmus and advancing into central Greece to meet Agesilaus. So the regent's army returned to Sparta. The allied army took a while to lick its wounds. Then, bloodied but unbowed, it proceeded to try its luck against Agesilaus.

Before this next encounter news arrived from the Aegean. Here a naval battle had been brewing for some time, although for a different war. The Persians, ably assisted by the Athenians, had started to gather a fleet in order to strike at the supply lines of the invading army which Agesilaus had expected to be leading deep into the Persian empire. The Spartan fleet had been mustered to prevent this. Thanks to developments on mainland Greece, Agesilaus' invasion had been cancelled and his army withdrawn. Now the role of the Spartan fleet was to stop the Persians and Athenians from recapturing the coastal and island cities that Agesilaus had left behind.

The combined fleet of Cypriots, Rhodians and Phoenicians was commanded by the highly competent and experienced admiral Conan the Athenian. This anti-Spartan alliance mustered ninety triremes and sundry minor vessels. Despite their many different nationalities, the crews of the different ships had this much in common: they were all experienced rowers. In the Spartan corner was an equal or just slightly smaller fleet, crewed by mercenary rowers and inexperienced Lacedaemonians. In command was the Spartan Peisander, whose qualification for taking on an experienced and battle-hardened enemy fleet was that he was the brother-in-law of Agesilaus.

Under the circumstances, it might be considered a victory for the Spartans if their fleet survived its first encounter with Conan, whose ships were aggressively seeking out the Spartan fleet. This was probably making an attempt to move north along the coast to accompany the king's army. The two fleets met near the Bay of Cermicus in south-west Anatolia, not far from the city of Cnidos which gives the subsequent battle its name. We have a short, confused and confusing account of what happened from Xenophon, who was himself no sailor.

It would appear that the advance vessels of Conan's fleet unexpectedly ran into the main Spartan fleet. Peisander promptly defeated these scouts and advanced on those which fled. This took him right into the main body of the combined allied fleet. This fell upon the disorganized Spartan advance like wolves on a flock of sheep. Peisander followed his equally unsuccessful predecessor Callimachus to a watery grave. After his death the surviving rowers in the Spartan fleet, desperate to get off the water, ran their ships onto the nearest beach and hurried inland. Thirty or so Spartan ships were destroyed in the naval action, but as triremes were designed to be beached regularly, those that had been run ashore were still in good shape. Consequently, Athens now added fifty captured triremes to its fleet and was well on the way to regaining its former naval glory.

For the Spartans, the experience of regularly raising and losing fleets was a disillusioning experience. It was also one which they could no longer afford, since Persia had stopped giving them money. They never took to the water again in any great force, and effectively abandoned their efforts to control Ionia. Conan and Pharnabazus now took themselves on an Aegean cruise. They stopped at every Spartan-controlled city along the way to turf Spartan appointees out of government, and they captured any Spartan garrisons that fell into their hands.

It is harder to find a real victory in the next act in the war which occurred in 394, not long after news of the Spartan defeat at Cnidos reached the mainland. This was the attempt of the allies to engage Agesilaus' veteran army as it advanced to Boeotia. There was one location where an army advancing from the north was most easily blocked. That was at Charonea, a place that has consequently witnessed several battles over the centuries.

This particular battle at Charonea looked at first to be a standard Spartan victory. The Spartans on the right were reinforced with many veterans of the march of the 10,000 who had originally joined the Spartan king in the hope of making another attempt at the Persian heartland. Together with the Spartans, they made up a powerful force of some 12,000 men, with the weakest component of the army – some 3,000 Orchomenans – arrayed, as custom dictated, on the left. Those facing the Spartans and mercenary veterans did not even stop to fight. As soon as they saw that the enemy was serious about combat these troops fled for safety. Agesilaus was already reorganizing his forces to resume his march when he discovered that on the other wing the Thebans had broken the hoplites from Orchomenus and were looting his baggage train. This included over a hundred talents of bullion looted during the Persian campaign, and the Spartans very much preferred that the Thebans did not get their hands on it.

What happened next is assumed to be because, for a number of reasons, Agesilaus really did not like the Thebans. It would have been easy enough for him to wheel his battle line and force the Thebans into a hasty withdrawal. This would have saved the baggage train and granted the Spartans a painless victory. Instead Agesilaus positioned his phalanx right across the Theban line of retreat. This meant that to get back to safety, the Thebans would have to fight their way through the Spartan army. Regardless of Agesilaus' personal animosity there was a good military case for crushing the Thebans. After all, there can be little doubt that Thebes was at the heart of the challenge to Spartan hegemony. Removing the cream of the Theban army would severely cripple that challenge.

It was Thebes which had encouraged the defection of Corinth from the Peloponnesian League and stirred up Thessaly. Above all, Thebes had restored the democracy in Athens – a democracy that was already pulling together the blocks of stone needed to restore its city's broken walls. The entire core of the Theban army was now in front of the king. The temptation to wipe it out entirely must have been irresistible to the Spartans, accustomed as they were to unflinchingly taking drastic measures no matter what the cost to others.

At Charonea, however, it was the Spartans themselves who were going to have to pay if they wanted to break Thebes. In fact, they were going to have to pay very dearly. The Thebans did not break, or even buckle. Instead, they fought back with a ferocity that impressed even the battle-hardened Spartans. What had seemed like an easy victory a few hours ago turned into anything but for Agesilaus. Caught in the thick of the fighting, he was only saved from death by the sacrifice of his fifty-man bodyguard. Even these men were so hard-pressed that they could not prevent the Thebans from inflicting a number of wounds on the king. In the end, the Spartans were forced to open their ranks to let the embattled Thebans through.

Given a line of retreat the Thebans gratefully took it. After that, although they suffered casualties along the way, the main body of Theban hoplites made it to safety. The next morning a battered and bandaged Agesilaus again offered battle, which the Thebans declined. In a way the battle had been a microcosm of what the Thebans had intended the war to prove all along: that they could go toe-to-toe with the Spartans and survive. Even if they did not win they could hold their own. Having painfully made that point the previous day, the Thebans had no intention of making it again. The historian Diodorus Siculus put the Theban casualties at 600 and those of the Spartans at 350. These might seem relatively trivial figures for a clash that involved somewhere around 35,000 men, but on the Spartan side most of the 350 who had fallen were Spartiates. These were the best the state had to offer, and men whom the Spartans could not afford to lose.

For the next five years hostilities continued but neither side had the strength to strike a decisive blow. Things were rather as they had been during the Peloponnesian War, with the Spartans unbeatable on land and their enemies supreme at sea. The major development of these years was that the alliance between Thebes and Corinth became so close that the two states removed the boundary stones between their territories and adopted a common government. This government was democratic, which sent a flood of outraged Corinthian aristocrats to Sparta and sparked some lively but inconclusive campaigning around Corinth.

It was becoming clear that as in the Peloponnesian War, Persian money was going to be the decisive factor. Accordingly both Spartans and Thebans began to court the Persians. They did so with an obsequiousness that would have sickened and stunned the Spartans who had fought the Persians at Thermopylae a century before.

The Spartans alleged that the Athenians under Conan were using their Persian-sponsored fleet to rebuild their Aegean empire. They also suggested a more general peace settlement on the basis that no Greek city should dominate another. The Athenians refused to settle on these terms, perhaps because they were indeed beginning to reassert their naval power. Secondly, the idea that no state should dominate another was rich coming from the Spartans who were a major power in Greece precisely because they dominated Messenia with brute force and terror.

The Persians were persuaded by the Spartan argument to the extent that the satrap Tiribazus arrested Conan (he later escaped). Otherwise they were so inclined towards the Theban side that Tibron, the exasperated Spartan leader in Asia Minor, started to treat the Persians as enemies. He ravaged Persian holdings until he was killed in an ambush. Naturally, the Greek cities of Ionia thoroughly approved of Tibron's activities and supported the Spartans, so for a while the Persian empire had a spirited brush-fire war in progress on its western borders.

It was probably this aggravation that finally persuaded the Persians to put serious pressure on Athens to end the war. The Persians had probably agreed with Sparta in advance that the current small war in Anatolia should end and control of the Greek cities of Asia Minor would be handed over to Persia in any peace deal. With the Spartans on board, Persia now presented the Athenians with an ultimatum: either make peace or face Sparta and Persia combined.

Athens and the allies had no choice but to back down from the combined Spartan–Persian menace. The Athenians were unwilling to run a reprise of the final stages of the Peloponnesian War, and the Thebans were aware that without Athenian ships they would have trouble containing Sparta, even with the support of Argos. This support was anyway less valuable than hoped. The Argive merger with Corinth was proving problematic, for the combined city-state was almost paralysed by political in-fighting.

In the end Sparta got what it wanted. The Thebans were forced to back out of their coalition and Athens was again cowed. Corinth was detached from Argos and again became a separate city, which was unwillingly once more co-opted by the Spartans into the Peloponnesian League. All it had taken for this Spartan 'victory' was handing the cities of Ionia back to the Persians. It was a good peace for the Spartans but hardly one in which they could take much pride. So obvious had been the power of Persian intervention, and so clearly did the final treaty favour Persia, that the treaty is sometimes called 'The King's Peace' after the Persian king who essentially dictated the terms. Sparta as a Persian lackey was not a good image for the city to present to the rest of Greece and as a result Spartan prestige fell yet further.

Persia was the outright winner in the Corinthian War. The threat of an invasion by Agesilaus had been removed, and Spartan armies had been withdrawn to the Greek mainland, where they had spent their time beating up and being savaged by other Greeks. Athens had been restored as a counterweight to Sparta but was too scared of Persia to be hostile. Above all, the Persians now had undisputed control of Ionia. With the Greek cities there firmly under Persian rule, troops could finally be spared to sort out anti-Persian rebellions in other places. These included Egypt, which was recaptured by Persian forces in 380 BC. True, in exchange Persia had to hand over domination of mainland Greece to the Spartans, but by the fourth century Persia had in any case abandoned plans to expand into Europe.

The Road to Leuctra

On the Greek mainland Sparta was now probably as powerful as the state had ever been, but there were two major differences between contemporary Sparta and the Sparta of a century before. The first was that until the Peloponnesian War Sparta had been admired and respected; after the Corinthian War Sparta was largely despised and feared. This did not bode well for a state that had one other major difference from the Sparta of earlier years: there were now far fewer Spartiates to enforce the nation's will. It did not help that the Spartans continued with the same block-headed approach to diplomacy that had provoked the Corinthian War in the first place. According to Xenophon: 'The Spartans decided to punish those allies who had been more inclined to their enemies in the recent war, and to put them into a situation where they could not again be disloyal.' (Xenophon, *Hellenica*, 5.2)

The first to suffer from this disciplinary policy were the people of Mantinea. Long a Spartan client, Mantinea stood accused of selling corn to Argos throughout the recent war, and also of not supplying troops on demand, fighting lackadaisically and then only when it was necessary. Consequently the Mantineans were ordered to pull down their walls and disperse into separate villages. When the people indignantly and not un-expectedly refused, Agesilaus arrived with an army to make it happen. The example of Mantinea was enough to make other members of the Pelo-ponnesian League acquiesce with whatever punishments Sparta saw fit to impose.

With the Peloponnesian League now united (though hardly loyal), Sparta could afford to expand its power in other directions. A successful campaign followed in Chalcidice in northern Greece, although the Spartans were affronted that the Thebans refused a request for troops to help them. This refusal had far-reaching consequences. The Spartan army had to pass by Thebes in order to get to and from northern Greece and on one such occasion a remarkable opportunity presented itself.

As was very common in Greek cities, Thebes had periodic bouts of civil strife. Now, seeing the Spartans nearby, the leaders of a particular faction approached the Spartan commander with an extraordinary offer. The Thebans were celebrating a festival called the Thesmophoria, and as part of that festival the Cadmeia of Thebes was turned over to the womenfolk of the city. The Cadmeia had the same role in Thebes as the Acropolis in Athens. It was the city's dominant geographical feature and religious centre. Also like the Acropolis, it was the city's fortress of last resort.

What the leader of the Theban renegades offered Phoibidas, the Spartan commander, was a chance to take this citadel and thus have Thebes at his mercy. All he wanted in exchange was to rule Thebes, and in that position to have the satisfaction of executing his enemies. Phoibidas took the offer and secretly led his men to capture the Cadmeia. Once the citadel was in Spartan hands, Phoibidas was master of the city – not least because in the process he had taken hostage all the leading women of Thebes. In one abrupt morning the second city of Greece, and Sparta's nearest rival, had suddenly become a Spartan puppet. This was a major coup but it would have severe repercussions.

Sparta's reputation for unflinching honesty and integrity had taken a beating after the city's cooperation with Persia during the Peloponnesian War. Sparta's stock had fallen still lower after the Corinthian War when it had basically handed over the cities of Ionia to Persia in exchange for dominance in the Greek mainland. Now Greece waited to see what Sparta would do about Phoibidas' conduct at Thebes.

It must be remembered that, firstly, Thebes had sworn a peace treaty with Sparta and had done nothing to violate those terms. The two states were not at war, and Thebes had not given any reason for war. Secondly, the taking of the Cadmeia had desecrated the proceedings of an important religious event. This was a major act of blasphemy which appalled the rest of Greece. Would the government of Sparta – which so frequently and vehemently proclaimed itself as the most god-fearing state in Greece – endorse this violation of the rites of Demeter?

The Spartan response was a measured exercise in hypocrisy. Phoibidas was put on trial for wanton aggression against a state with which Sparta was not at war. Secondly, he was tried for sacrilege in that he had violated the rites of Demeter (which was by no means a lesser charge). At this trial King Agesilaus himself led the defence. Spartan commanders, he argued, were always trained to act in Sparta's best interests while they were in the field. Therefore what those conducting the trial should be asking was not whether what Phoibidas had done was right or wrong, but whether it was in Sparta's best interests that he had acted as he had. If what he had done was in Sparta's best interests, as it demonstrably was, then the man had simply been following the standard instructions given to every commander in the field, and no Spartan should be punished for following orders.

In the end, despite the efforts of Agesilaus, Phoibidas was found guilty, but this was little more than a sop to outraged public opinion in Greece. He was given a small fine and temporarily retired from public life (he later returned in a position of command when it was reckoned the fuss had died down). Thereafter the Spartans maintained that, although what Phoibidas had done was wrong, what he had done was done and there was no going back. A Spartan garrison would remain on the Cadmeia. Plutarch remarks, 'This showed the Greeks an amazing inconsistency. They punished the wrong-doer but endorsed what he had done.' (Plutarch, *Pelopidas*, 6)

The devout Xenophon was in no doubt that this decision was the immediate cause of the fall of Sparta:

> The Gods unfailingly take note of wickedness and impious deeds ... The Spartans, who had sworn to leave the states [of Greece] autonomous, seized possession of the Cadmeia of Thebes. For this they were punished, and by the very people whom they had so wronged.
>
> (Xenophon, *Hellenica*, 5.4.1)

If the devout and unreservedly pro-Spartan Xenophon felt this way, then there can be little doubt that many Spartans felt the same, quite apart from the outrage in the rest of Greece. The Spartans had violated the oaths they had sworn at the end of the Corinthian War. Everyone knew it; just as importantly the Spartans knew it, and the Spartans genuinely were a god-fearing people. It could not have been a pleasant feeling for Spartans subsequently going into battle, knowing that they had offended their gods and that the punishment for this was still pending.

For the next four years an uneasy peace endured over mainland Greece, the only exception being a successful Spartan action against the city of Olynthus in the north. The situation in Thebes was particularly tense, because the Theban people resented Spartan domination and the puppet government that served the Spartans. It did not help that just over the Cytherean mountains in Attica was a core of democratic exiles who had fled Thebes at the time of the Spartan takeover. The Athenians were grateful to these men for their role in restoring the Athenian democracy and obdurately continued to protect them, even in the face of Spartan demands for their return and an assassination attempt by the Theban government. Finally, the exiles struck back.

The government in Thebes had been growing steadily more repressive and tyrannical, secure in the knowledge that the Spartan garrison on the Cadmeia would protect them from retaliation for any atrocities. Accordingly, someone suggested a party at which the top men in the Theban government would be 'entertained' by the wives and daughters of the leading men of the city. After horrified protests, it was agreed that the party would go ahead, but in order to protect the good name of the ladies involved no servants would be present. Furthermore, the ladies would arrive cloaked and veiled so that no one would know their identities until they were alone in the dining hall with the Theban leaders. These were, as Plutarch drily remarks, 'looking forward to a pleasant evening'.

When the moment for the unveiling came, it was revealed that the young flesh beneath the cloaks was male, armed and not at all romantically inclined. Fortunately the party had been planned for a while, so the assassins had time to coordinate their actions with the Athenians, whose army showed up outside Thebes just as the Thebans discovered that their current leaders were dead. This put the Spartan garrison on the Cadmeia in a difficult position. They could probably deal with the rebellious people of Thebes or with an Athenian army, but not both together.

Eventually the Spartan garrison commander negotiated a deal by which he and his men would be able to leave unmolested. However, the safe passage of this agreement very definitely did not apply to the former lackeys of the Theban tyranny who had sought shelter with the Spartans. They were pulled out of the ranks of the departing garrison and killed on the spot. Such was the hatred felt for the tyranny that had been imposed upon them that the mob also killed the wives and even the children of their former oppressors.

The Spartans were not going to take this lying down. For a start they executed the commander of the garrison on the Cadmeia for abandoning his post, and then they sent an army into Boeotia. Significantly, this army was not commanded by Agesilaus. The Ephors doubtless felt that his well-known dislike of the Thebans was likely to cause more problems than it solved. Instead the current Eurypontid king, a man called Cleombrotus, was put in command.

Cleombrotus did not achieve very much on his campaign, other than to sponsor a foolhardy attempt to seize the Piraeus in Athens rather in the manner that Phoibidas had seized the Cadmeia in Thebes. The coup failed, much to Spartan embarrassment, and the Spartans duly prosecuted the man who had led the attempt. (Thanks to the intervention of Agesilaus, he was acquitted.) Cleombrotus, the man who had instigated the attack, was not charged but he was discredited. Command of the war against Thebes was transferred to Agesilaus, who was determined that the phony war fought by his predecessor was over.

The ill-judged raid against Athens also had another consequence. The Athenians regretted their support for Thebes to such an extent that they had killed one of the generals who led the attack on the Cadmeia and forced the other into exile. Now, as it appeared that this back-tracking had failed to appease the Spartans, the Athenians took the opposite direction and allied themselves with the Thebans. This mattered because the Athenians had managed to build themselves a handy little confederation of allies. Athenian diplomacy had been at pains to make clear that this new alliance was a partnership of equals and that there would be no return to the days of Athenian domination by the Delian League. As a result of this persuasion the city had acquired allies in Euboea and among those few cities in Ionia that were not under Persian domination.

The Thebans were not prepared to take on Sparta in a head-on battle. For the first year they devoted their efforts to limiting the attempts of Agesilaus to plunder their lands. When the king departed he left in command of the army on Boeotia none other than the supposedly disgraced Phoibidas who had caused the entire problem in the first place by capturing the Cadmeia. Phoibidas continued Spartan depredations on Theban land until the exasperated Thebans gathered an army and marched on the city of Thespiae, which the Spartans had been using as their base. Since Agesilaus had taken much of the Spartan army home with him, Phoibidas had been relying on mercenary peltasts and Thespian hoplites. These forced the Thebans into retreat, but when the Theban cavalry turned on them the mercenaries broke and Phoibidas was killed. Those so inclined in Greece quietly noted the first score in Demeter's revenge for the violation of her rites.

The next campaigning season saw Agesilaus back in Boeotia and even more determined to inflict serious pain upon the Thebans. However, the Thebans were equally determined to avoid battle unless it was to be fought on ground that favoured them. His previous experience had given Agesilaus too much respect for the Theban infantry to fight on those terms, so there was no clash of armies. Instead another war dragged into stalemate. Agesilaus was now into his sixties and in poor health. With Agesilaus unable to campaign in the following years, hostilities were led by Cleombrotus. He campaigned with such a marked lack of hostility that at one point his men asked him if they were actually still at war.

Stalled on land, the Spartans attempted to prise the Athenians away from their alliance with Thebes by making things difficult at sea. In response the Athenians crushed a nascent Spartan naval revival at Naxos, where they sank or captured most of the Spartan fleet. The upshot of the war at sea was that this convincing demonstration of Athenian power brought her alliance up to some seventy cities, both major and (mostly) minor. By now there was a general sentiment in Greece that Sparta was failing. The Spartans needed a convincing demonstration to show that they were still the dominant power in Greece. Regrettably, their efforts to provide this demonstration had completely the opposite effect.

Chapter 9

The Disaster at Leuctra

Pelopidas and Epaminondas

One of the problems with the Spartan kingship – accurately diagnosed by Lysander, and before that by the regent Pausanias – was that it was hereditary. This certainly prevented most power struggles, since there were generally only one or two candidates available for the position of king in each of the two royal lines. On the other hand, it meant that those not of royal blood, even if best suited for power, ran into a bronze ceiling when it came to taking the top job.

In Athens, by contrast, a Pericles or a Thrasybulus could rise to lead the state, and be ruthlessly done away with by the electorate if he failed to live up to expectations. In Sparta whether or not a king was competent depended on a roll of the genetic dice. Competent or not, once chosen a king tended to stay in power until he died or his incompetence caused him to be exiled (by which time the damage had generally been done). As a result of the Spartan kingship system, Sparta had something of a leadership deficit at this critical juncture in her fortunes. Currently the state was led by an elderly man in poor health and a colleague who had proven himself to be at best reluctant to fight and at worst positively timid.

Meanwhile, in royalty-free Thebes a dynamic duo had risen to lead the state. These were two aristocrats who had worked closely together ever since one of them, Epaminondas, had saved the life of the other, Pelopidas, in an obscure battle near Mantinea. (Possibly the pair were serving in a Theban contingent summoned by Agesilaus to take part in his police action against Mantinea at the end of the Corinthian War.) Both men were democratic supporters and had fled to Athens after the Spartan takeover of the Cadmeia. As leaders of the exiles, the pair were instrumental in devising the plot that led to the demise of the Theban leadership and the restoration of the Theban democracy. It was Pelopidas and Epaminondas who urged patience in the face of repeated Spartan invasions that ravaged Theban territory. Perhaps the pair realized that with these invasions the Spartans were breaking one of their own professed rules of warfare: that they should not campaign against any single state for several years in a row, lest the people of that state become familiar with Spartan warfare and accustomed to fighting their army.

By now Thebes had been fighting Sparta on and off for almost a generation. During the period of the Spartan occupation of the Cadmeia the Thebans had been forced to fight alongside the Spartans in northern Greece – an experience which had shown them the Spartan military machine from the inside. To counter the king's elite Spartiate bodyguard the Thebans formed an equivalent body of 300 elite hoplites, later known as the Sacred Band. In later years it was held that the Sacred Band consisted of 150 pairs of male lovers who fought side by side and preferred death to dishonouring their love through cowardice or defeat.

Some modern historians have expressed scepticism that the Band was so formed, given that it contrasted sharply with the norms of Greek military deployment and homosexual relationships. However, contemporary Greek historians seem to have accepted the composition of the Band as a given fact, and in the absence of countervailing evidence we shall do the same here. In any case, the important thing about the Band is not the romantic disposition of its members but the fact that these men made up a hard core of trained soldiers who drilled regularly. These men achieved a military competence equal to the best that Sparta had to offer and this was emulated, albeit to a lesser extent, by the rest of the Theban army. Even without the example of the Band, repeated clashes with the Spartans were turning the Theban army into a veteran corps.

> This is the reason for what Antalcidas the Spartan said to Agesilaus when he returned from Boeotia wounded in battle. 'That's the fee the Thebans are paying their teacher, since you are instructing them in war, even though they did not wish to fight.' (Plutarch, *Pelopidas*, 15)

The Battle of Orchomenus (Tegyra), 375

It has already been seen that Charonea occupied a strategic site in Boeotia. The same was true of Orchomenus, a small town not far from Charonea to the east. When Pelopidas learned that the Spartan garrison in Orchomenus had left to take part in operations further to the north, the Theban leader decided to see if he could retake this important position. The plan failed because, while still *en route* to Orchomenus, Pelopidas discovered that the Spartans had reinforced the city with fresh troops from Laconia to make up for the men absent in the north.

While withdrawing to Thebes Pelopidas ran into those same Spartan forces which had been deployed in the north. They had completed their operations and were returning to Orchomenus. The result was less of a planned battle than a violent collision. It is clear that the Spartans were not deployed for battle as accounts describe the *polemarchs*, the Spartan unit commanders, as being close together. This must mean that they were at the head of parallel columns because if their phalanx had been deployed, the *polemarchs* would have been some distance apart. The Spartan forces considerably outnumbered the Thebans, who seem to have had the advantage of better scouting. This meant that although Pelopidas had no chance of avoiding battle, he had a few crucial extra minutes in which to prepare for it. When one of the Thebans fearfully commented that they had fallen right into the hands of the Spartans, Pelopidas snapped back, 'And why have they not fallen into ours?'

The key to the battle would be to hit the Laconians before they could get set. There were just 300 Thebans, almost certainly the Sacred Band, with a goodly number of cavalry in support. How many Spartans were present is uncertain. Plutarch quotes his sources as giving the different figures of 500, 700 and 900, and we also do not know how many of these were Spartiates, other Laconians or Orchomenan allies. However, there was at least a substantial Spartan contingent, and it is probable that difference in numbers is because some contemporary historians were interested only in hoplites and did not bother counting auxiliary troops. Therefore a provisional guess might be that 500 Spartans (at most) and 200 others faced a force of 300 Thebans plus light troops and cavalry.

Pelopidas ordered his cavalry immediately into the attack and ordered the Band to follow close behind. This is another indication that the Spartans were not properly set because a cavalry charge against a formed hoplite line is pointless, and achieves nothing other than to kill off the cavalry contingent. As it was it seems that the cavalry hit the *polemarchs* as they were organizing their lines, and both men were slain. And hard on the heels of the cavalry came the 300 of the Band, formed up in good order.

The Spartans assumed that the Thebans intended to seek safety as they had done at Charonea, so they opened their ranks to let the charging hoplites through. But instead the Thebans stood and fought, making selective charges against any Spartan units that looked as though they might be struggling into proper formation. Leaderless, disorganized and startled by the suddenness and ferocity of the attack, the Spartan force broke and fled for the safety of nearby Orchomenus.

This was a remarkable victory for the Thebans. At Sphacteria in the Peloponnesian War a force of Spartan hoplites had been defeated by light troops using irregular tactics, and at Charonea the Thebans had for a while fought toe-to-toe with the Spartans and not disgraced themselves. But here at Tegyra a smaller force of Thebans had put a superior number of Spartans to flight. Plutarch sums up the significance of this victory:

> The Lacedaemonians had never before been overpowered by an enemy whom they outnumbered. They had not even been beaten in battle when the armies were evenly matched. Because of this when it came to close combat the Spartan morale was irresistibly high, while their enemies were terrified by the Spartan reputation alone and thought themselves outmatched. It was this battle [at Tegyra] that first taught the other Greeks that unbeatable fighters did not have to be reared on the banks of the Eurotas [the Eurotas being the river that flowed past Sparta]. (Plutarch, *Pelopidas*, 17)

Some time after this the Spartans made a half-hearted effort to reassert their naval power. They decided to start this project on the west coast of Greece, well away from the Athenians. Scraping up a force of sixty triremes from their allies they set about taking the island city of Corcyra where disaffected local aristocrats had promised to hand over to the Spartans if they arrived with sufficient force. Although the Spartans claimed that their fleet was merely stopping on a goodwill visit en route to Sicily the Corcyran democracy was not fooled. The leaders immediately sent to Athens for help and refused to open their gates to the visitors. Thereupon the Spartans dropped all pretence and began an active attack on the city.

The siege did not go well. The Spartan force suffered from poor discipline, mostly due to lack of pay. Since the Spartan commander had been given plenty of funds for the operation, there are good grounds for supposing that this man was intent on embezzling the better part of the men's pay for himself. When a well-armed and trained Athenian force arrived to help their allies, they found that the Corcyrans had already disposed of the demoralized Spartan force for themselves with one well-timed sally. The Spartan commander had been killed, and the fleet had taken what booty it had obtained thus far and dispersed to its home ports. It was an inglorious end to a disreputable enterprise. Yet again the invincible Spartans had revealed feet of clay.

At this point the war became bogged down into a series of minor actions mixed with complex inter-city politics. Finally, in 371 BC the Persians intervened. They rather liked the current status quo in Greece, and their calculated interventions on each side were aimed at keeping the Greeks equal and at each other's throats. However, they did not want the Greeks so debilitated that one or the other state might collapse completely into the power of another.

The Persians did not want Sparta to fall. Equally they did not want Sparta to obliterate Thebes, leaving no counterweight to an increasingly self-confident Athens. And they certainly did not want Athens and Sparta combining forces against Thebes. (This last was also possible because although Thebes and Athens were currently allies, the Athenians were becoming uneasy about the way Thebes was subordinating the rest of Boeotia to its power.) It was time, the Persians reckoned, for everyone to step back and take a deep breath.

The growing self-confidence of the Athenians was shared by the Thebans. When presented with a peace treaty to sign, Pelopidas insisted on signing not for Thebes alone as before, but on behalf of the Boeotians in general. Since the Spartans wanted the cities of Greece to be autonomous, they naturally refused to let one city speak for an entire region. However, on the Theban side acknowledging the independence of the cities of Boeotia would undo all the gains Thebes had made in gaining control of the region and this they were loath to do.

Therefore, when told that each Boeotian city should sign for itself, Pelopidas replied that he did not see any Messenian delegates present to sign for their oppressed people. The Spartan argument that their occupation of Messenia was a special case was rejected as blatant hypocrisy, and the peace talks broke up in acrimony. However, Spartan diplomacy did exert itself at this conference to the point where the Spartans were able to make peace with the other cities of Greece. This diplomatic success meant that Thebes was now the sole focus of Sparta's malignant attention.

From the Spartan point of view it was definitely time to do something about Thebes. If this could not be accomplished by diplomacy, no matter. The Spartans were in any case more comfortable asserting their will on the battlefield. Accordingly, Cleombrotus marched north with a substantial Spartan army. So urgently did the Spartans feel the need to discipline the Thebans that they ignored those who advised that yet again the Spartans were not practising what they preached. If they advocated the autonomy of Greek cities then they should consult their allies. Then those who wanted to join the campaign could send troops (or, as the army was already mustered, those who wanted no part in this fight should be given the chance to withdraw their troops).

In their eagerness to get to war the Spartan leadership disregarded this counsel and immediately marched north with the army they had. This proved a crucial error for it meant that the Spartan army went to war with a built-in Achilles heel of allies who did not want to be there. Certainly these reluctant conscripts did not want to face those same disciplined, highly motivated Thebans who had beaten the Spartans at Tegyra.

Leuctra, 371 BC

Many years ago, and long before the Theban and Spartan armies met at that place, legend claimed that other Spartans and Thebans had an unfortunate encounter at Leuctra, a small village some 10 kilometres from Thebes. A band of young Spartans had come across a man called Scedasus who was escorting his daughters on a journey. The young men had attacked the group and raped and murdered the girls. The father made repeated representations to the Spartans asking for justice, but all his pleas were ignored. Finally he put the matter in the hands of the gods by heaping curses on the Spartans even as he killed himself beside the tombs of his children.

Thereafter, 'Beware the wrath of Leuctra' was a common prophecy in Sparta. However, there were several places in Greece called Leuctra and many dire prophecies floating about, most of which did not come true. So in this case the Spartans paid no heed until recognition came well after the event.

Cleombrotus arrived at Leuctra by crossing to Boeotia from further east than expected. This caused some consternation among the Thebans, who had been waiting at Charonea. Theban alarm was all the greater because Cleombrotus' approach appeared to be showing unprecedented signs of military acumen and because the Spartan army was larger than expected. (As usual, different sources give different figures, but the best estimate is Plutarch's assessment of around 9,000 on the Theban side, and 10,000 on the Spartan side. Importantly, the 'Spartan side' was very far from being all Spartan, and the Theban side contained many allies – willing or not – from the rest of Boeotia.)

Given how crucial the events at Leuctra were to subsequent Spartan history it is regrettable that our sources are so imprecise. Plutarch was no military man and he treats the battle in a single paragraph. Xenophon was a military man and more than capable of providing an expert analysis, but he was also very pro-Spartan and it evidently causes him great pain to mention the battle at all. (The previous battle at Tegyra he passes over in disdainful silence.) Therefore we have to fall back on the account of Diodorus Siculus, who seems more interested in the various portents and prophecies beforehand than in the battle itself.

For the protagonists at the time the Spartan army was a known quantity. The generalship of Cleombrotus would be solid and uninspired and the battle-worthiness of the Spartan hoplites was beyond question. Thus it became clear that the battle would depend on two unknown factors on the Theban side. It remained to be seen what Epaminondas could do as a general, and no one knew how the somewhat unnerved Theban army would acquit itself in battle.

The core of that army was the 300 of the Sacred Band. If that number does not seem very high, it should be noted that the core of the Spartan army – the Spartiates – numbered just 700. As Aristotle was to remark later, this was an astonishing drop in the number of Spartans from the size of the armies put into the field just a few generations before. The rest of the Spartan army comprised *perioiki*, lesser Spartans, and allies.

The allies had been fighting Thebans, Athenians and others for almost a decade now while Sparta attempted to maintain its hegemony of Greece through brute force. That this attempt had failed was evident from the fact that the allies were now being compelled to fight yet again – and it was not a task they contemplated with enthusiasm.

The early skirmishing of the battle went in favour of Sparta's veteran mercenary peltasts. It seems that the Thebans were using part-timers in this role: baggage porters, carters and others from the baggage train. Defeated by the Spartan skirmishers, these light irregular troops started to withdraw to nearby Thebes. The Spartans kept pressing, which was a mistake. Hieron, the Spartan commander of the light troops, was killed and the irregular Theban skirmishers were forced back to swell the numbers of the main Theban army.

Meanwhile Cleombrotus took the opportunity to survey the Theban deployment. He noted that the formation of hoplites on the Theban left was unusually deep. His own men were in the standard formation of twelve ranks deep, while the Thebans seemed to have chosen to be at least three times deeper. This deep deployment was usually a sign of a lack of confidence in a phalanx's fighting ability. Apart from the men in the front ranks, the rest of the phalanx was there to add mass and to make it harder for those doing the actual fighting to break and run.

Because the Thebans had formed up so deep and were fewer in the first place, there was a considerable overlap on the Spartan left flank. The Spartan king accordingly and predictably moved his troops on that flank forwards and sideways in an outflanking manoeuvre. Epaminondas had foreseen this and unleashed his cavalry, which force was at this time perhaps the best in Greece. We do not know for certain who the Spartans were using for cavalry nor how many there were. We do know that the horsemen deployed by Cleombrotus failed to stop the Theban charge. As it fell back, the defeated cavalry was funnelled through the gap left in the Spartan line by Cleombrotus' attempted outflanking manoeuvre. This caused considerable disorder among both the outflanking troops and the main body of the Spartan phalanx.

Meanwhile Epaminondas had two further innovations for the startled Cleombrotus to consider. Firstly, the Theban commander had deployed his best troops not on the right, as was traditional, but on the left so that they would be facing the Spartan king and his best men. Secondly, the army advanced obliquely, moving slightly to the left, and with blocks of troops in the centre and right wing holding back. These – in another innovation – were screened by skirmishers and cavalry to prevent the rest of the Spartan army from engaging prematurely with them.

In this echelon formation the first Thebans to hit the Spartan line were the elite Sacred Band as the spear-tip of the deep phalanx on the left. While the rest of the Theban army had hung back, these men had been closing in extraordinarily fast. Epaminondas had learned the lesson of Tegyra, that infantry can be highly effective when following close behind cavalry that had disrupted the opposition formations. Now the sheer weight of the deep Theban formation simply pushed the Spartan line aside, while the Theban unit retained its shape.

The Spartan allied hoplites on the left had not yet engaged because the rest of the Theban army had not yet come up to their battle line. Therefore these stunned troops were treated to a sight never before seen, and in fact heretofore inconceivable: a formed and prepared battle line of Spartiates broken by an enemy charge. Not only that but the commander, King Cleombrotus, was killed while his men were being overwhelmed. That was more than enough for the Spartan allies, many of whom had not wanted to be there in the first place. They had not yet engaged the Thebans and now declined to do so and withdrew from the field. Essentially the defeat of the Spartiate right by the elite Theban left had already decided the battle – and very clearly not in Sparta's favour.

The Spartans, typically, did not recognize that they had been beaten. There is a limit to how much push even a very deep phalanx formation can muster (and this has been shown by practical research to be much less than assumed by previous generations of historians). Therefore, although they had lost probably more than half their number in that first chaotic engagement, the Spartans managed to pull their phalanx together and form an organized battle line in front of their camp. There was not another army in Greece that could have achieved this, let alone be ready and willing to keep fighting after what they had gone through. But it was not enough. The 300 Spartiate survivors might have been ready to keep fighting and some of the shell-shocked Lacedaemonians might have stuck with them, but the rest of Sparta's allies were done. They were not coming back to the battle, leaving the reluctant but heavily outnumbered Spartans no choice but to withdraw. The Spartans had to ask the Thebans for permission to collect their dead – a request which constituted formal acknowledgement that they had lost the battle. Plutarch estimates the overall Spartan casualties at around a thousand. (Plutarch, *Agesilaus*, 28)

Thereafter the Spartans marched from the field, a process they accomplished with relative ease because the Thebans still did not fully appreciate the extent of their victory, or the degree to which the Spartan allies were reluctant to fight. In fact the Thebans were still outnumbered and given better morale and motivation on the Spartan side the result of the battle might have been very different. However, the allies had seen the Spartiates broken, even if only temporarily. That single fact not only determined the battle, it also determined the fate of the Peloponnesian League and the future of Sparta.

In acknowledgement of the significance of this victory the Thebans set up a trophy – a formal structure showing that they claimed the battlefield. These trophies were usually temporary things, but in this particular case the Thebans made theirs of stone. They intended it to be a permanent reminder to the rest of Greece that the Spartans were not invincible.

Aftershocks

The Spartan government received the grim news of their defeat on the last days of the religious festival of the Gymnopaidea. This being Sparta, the festival continued to its end without a hitch and the mothers and wives of the fallen were told to postpone their grief. Then the surviving king, Agesilaus, sat down with the Ephors to decide what to do next. The first issue was that the shocking lack of Spartiates was now inescapably obvious.

It has been estimated that before Leuctra there were around 1,400 Spartiates capable of taking the field (*see* Godfrey Hutchinson, *Sparta; Unfit for Empire*, Frontline Books, 2014). Some 400 of these had fallen at Leuctra. If proper Spartan procedure were to be followed the surviving 300 in that army should now lose their citizenship. They were *tresantes* – literally 'runners away': cowards who had withdrawn from the battlefield. This would leave the city with a grand total of 700 Spartiates – somewhat less than the 10,000 that Sparta could field in its prime. This was so unacceptable that Agesilaus decreed that 'the laws should sleep for a day'. The 300 survivors kept their Spartiate status and the question of systemic reform to address the underlying problem was ducked yet again.

Now came the next question. How would the Thebans follow up their victory, and what was to be done in response? In the first months after the battle the Theban leaders made no moves directly against Sparta. They were busily mopping up Sparta's last allies in Boeotia, undoing Sparta's gains in the Chersonese, and consolidating their city's position as the leading state in Greece. Even the island of Euboea came under the Theban hegemony, much to the shock and indignation of the Athenians who had always considered the island within their sphere of influence. Agesilaus made use of the breathing space to make a military incursion into Elis, in the north-western Peloponnese, but he fought no major engagement and the demonstration was purely to restore Spartan morale.

It might be noted that in previous years Thebes had taken a beating at Nemea and again at Charonea yet had readily bounced back ready for another round against Sparta. Yet Sparta, having taken but the single body-blow at Leuctra, was almost a spent force. There were two reasons for this. One was that it was very easy for a family to drop from the rank of Spartiate, but there was no corresponding mechanism by which an ambitious clan might rise to that rank. As a result the men lost at Leuctra and in other battles both major and minor over the past decade had not been replaced.

It is possible to argue that Sparta was defeated by its own social system. Leuctra was not even a symptom – it was an inevitability. If the Spartans had not been defeated at Leuctra, their low and declining numbers, combined with their ambition to be masters of Greece, meant that reality would have caught up with the city elsewhere, and sooner rather than later. As a modern historian has remarked, after Leuctra 'Sparta broke, because Sparta was already fragile' (W.G. Forrest, *History of Sparta*, Bristol Classical Press, 1998, p. 167).

The second factor preventing a Spartan recovery was that the Peloponnesian League had collapsed. It had existed largely as a result of Spartan coercion and once Sparta lacked the power to coerce, the allies deserted the Spartan cause with a certain degree of relief. After all, these allies had lost almost a generation of young men in fighting Persians, Thebans and the cities of the Chersonese in northern Greece, and all for the benefit of Sparta rather than themselves. Opting out of the Peloponnesian League meant opting out of Sparta's seemingly interminable wars. After Leuctra all the allies had jumped ship together, so there was no way Sparta could bring the collective force of the League to bear on individual deserters.

Mantinea demonstrated this almost immediately. The city had been broken by the Spartans for lack of commitment to that city's cause during the Corinthian War. Since Sparta could no longer stop them, the Mantineans set about restoring their city and rebuilding the walls that Agesilaus had thrown down. The Mantineans did this with a certain degree of trepidation, knowing that as soon as it could regain its strength Sparta would certainly react violently to such insubordination. Therefore Mantinea was instrumental in creating a new league out of Sparta's former Peloponnesian allies.

This league became known as the Arcadian League, and this league and the Achaean League which followed were to remain a factor in the history of Greece until the Roman conquest two centuries later. As intended, the new league provided a counterweight to Spartan ambitions in the Peloponnese. The manpower that Sparta had once relied upon to beef up armies short of Spartiates was henceforth unavailable to a city now desperately short of hoplites. In fact, in any foreseeable future clash it was likely that Sparta's former allies would be fighting on the other side.

These two factors – the lack of Spartiates and the loss of the Peloponnesian League – made it impossible for Sparta to stage the sort of recovery that Thebes had managed after that city's defeats in the Corinthian War, or indeed to match the comeback made by Athens after that city had been totally crushed in the Peloponnesian War of a generation before. Furthermore, Pelopidas and Epaminondas had no intention of sitting back and letting Sparta recover. They intended to hit their enemies while they were down and to keep on hitting until they could not get up again.

Accordingly, in the year 370 BC the peoples of Laconia were treated to a sight that no one had seen for over three centuries: an invading army. This army was far from being Theban alone. The Arcadians were there, as were the Phocians. The Thessalians sent cavalry and volunteers came from Euboea. Contingents also came from Locris, Elis and Argos. The only two cities which held back were Athens, through dislike of an over-mighty Thebes, and Corinth which was still technically a Spartan ally.

Even without these two cities the invaders represented the largest and most diverse army assembled in Greece since the Persian Wars. That previous army had mustered under Spartan leadership to throw back the Persian invasion; the current army had united under Theban leadership to invade and destroy Sparta. It was fitting that decades of diplomatic mismanagement and brutal arrogance by the Spartan government should culminate in Laconia being invaded by the peoples of the Greek nation whom the Spartans had united against themselves. Perhaps Delphi had been right to warn Sparta that she would be 'brought low by a lame king'.

Sparta's women certainly lamented the city's lack of walls. In fact, they lamented so loudly that their distress caused considerable annoyance to Agesilaus, who was waiting with his men in grim silence as they prepared for the final defence of their city. However, nature provided the protection which the Spartans had failed to give themselves. The rains that year were unusually heavy, and having convened at Sellasia, the invaders had proceeded south, looting and burning along the east bank of the river Eurotas. When they came level with Sparta, they discovered that either the Spartans or the swollen river had destroyed the bridges and there was no way to get to the enemy city. The army had to proceed to Amyklai before a fordable site was reached.

By that time Corinth and some of Sparta's few remaining Peloponnesian allies had managed to send reinforcements, which came trailing in behind the invading army. Furthermore, the Ephors had foreseen that Sparta would desperately need manpower in the weeks after Leuctra and they had turned to the only untapped source remaining. They promised freedom to any helot who volunteered to fight for Sparta. Such was the desperation of helots to be freed of Spartan oppression that no fewer than 6,000 of them leapt at the chance. Sparta suddenly had the men, but more than one Spartan looked uneasily at the massed ranks of armed helots and wondered, when push came to shove, which side they would be fighting for.

Wisely, Epaminondas did not force the issue. He kept the army moving south to devastate the Spartan port of Glytheon. In the process he peeled away successive communities of *perioiki* from their alliance with Sparta. Then in the most brutal blow of all Epaminondas led his army into Messenia. The looting here was limited and only of clearly Spartan possessions. At this point Epaminondas was genuinely leading an army of liberation. He took his men to Mount Ithome, the spiritual heart of Messenian resistance to Spartan domination, and fortified the place as it had never been fortified before. Then the peoples of the surrounding countryside were invited to declare themselves free of Spartan rule and to take over Spartan possessions.

The new city of Messene was founded in the shadow of Mount Ithome, and Messenian exiles were given an open invitation to return to their motherland and settle there. After almost 600 years of savage and continual oppression the Messenians were no longer helots. Since they were by definition freed already, the helots who had been mustered to fight for Sparta took their leave of their former masters and returned to their now-liberated homeland. It is not recorded whether they took their weapons with them, but one thing was very clear: if the Spartans wanted Messenia back they would have to reconquer the place from scratch, just as they had done in the last years of the Archaic era.

There was also another issue. The conquest of Messenia in the Archaic era had doubled Spartan territory and pushed the state to become one of the top cities in Greece. Without Messenia Sparta was once again a second-rank city which lacked the resources and allies that such a reconquest would require.

Setting up Messenian defences and a government for a people unaccustomed to freedom took time; Epaminondas and Pelopidas took that time and did it right. In fact, they took so much time that they returned late to Thebes after holding their commands for six months too long. For this, jealous rivals in Thebes prosecuted the pair who had to stand trial for their lives. However, what they had achieved was simply too great for even the most petty-minded and spiteful juror to ignore. Before Leuctra, Sparta had been the dominant power in Greece. By the end of the campaign of 370, Sparta was a hollow reputation with about as much actual power as, say, Mantinea.

However, the actual war was far from over. Sparta itself may have been reduced to the rank of a second-rate city but still had as allies the first-rank cities of Corinth and Syracuse. To these formidable powers was now added the strength of Athens. Here again we see how inter-city rivalry tended to level the power of Greek cities. As Thebes now seemed overly powerful, Athens immediately joined with her old rival Sparta in order to rein in the Thebans. Nor would Corinth ever relinquish the alliance with Sparta while Argos was so closely aligned with Thebes. The Athenians had in fact attempted to act in concert with Corinth to block the return of Thebes and its allies from the Peloponnese, but this first Athenian action on the Spartan side was easily foiled by the veteran Theban troops.

The years since the Peloponnesian War had seen Corinth allied with Athens against Sparta, Thebes and Athens aligned against Sparta, and Sparta and Corinth allied against Thebes. This ever-shifting kaleidoscope of alliances was a part of the Greek political landscape, so the fact that Athens and Sparta were now working in tandem against Thebes was both ephemeral and ultimately irrelevant. The significant, tectonic shifts were that the Peloponnesian League had been permanently broken and re-formed into an essentially anti-Spartan confederation, and half of Sparta's territory had gone with Messenian independence – and the richer, more fertile, half at that. These latter changes constituted a permanent change in the political landscape of Greece.

Chapter 10

The Rise of Macedon

Due to political complications to the north, the kingdom of Macedon had given to the Thebans a young hostage as a warranty for the kingdom's good behaviour. That hostage was the son of the Macedonian king, but as he was a younger son with two older brothers ahead of him in the line of succession he was evidently reckoned disposable. As always with such hostages, the young man was somewhere between a prisoner and an honoured guest. He resided in the house of one Pammenes and was frequently in the company of Epaminondas and Pelopidas during the years when they broke Spartan power. The young man was a quick learner and even more than others in Greece he quickly appreciated what the Thebans had done and how they had done it.

As it turned out, even the king's third son was needed by the Macedonians, since the troubled times in their kingdom got through the two older brothers in short order. One was assassinated and the other died in battle with the Illyrians. Although he originally returned to become regent for the infant son of one of his brothers, the former hostage quickly established himself as king and began to rule Macedon as Philip II. At the time no one paid much attention to this development.

Arcadia and the Spartans

Meanwhile, to the south Greece continued with round after round of the ceaseless warfare that was impoverishing the land of manpower, crops and finances. The Thebans staged another invasion of the Peloponnese, which achieved little other than further devastating lands not yet recovered from the previous round of devastation. There is a story (related by the commentator Theopompus and relayed through Plutarch) that Theban magistrates had already concluded that this second invasion had achieved the little it was going to achieve. They were discussing their withdrawal when a secret envoy came from the Spartans offering ten talents of gold to the Thebans if they departed. In consequence the Thebans were in the happy position of being well paid for something they were going to do anyway.

It is uncertain whether this bribe was offered on the occasion of the first or second invasion, and whether this second invasion or the first was in response to the earnest desire of the Spartans to break up the new Arcadian League. Agesilaus had incurred the wrath of the Thebans when he marched north to prevent the building of the new Arcadian city of Megalopolis. This city was ever more to be a thorn in the Spartan side for it occupied a large valley just above the Taygetos range. This valley was one of the easier ways to move an army from Sparta to Messenia, and was all the more important because the Messenians had studied their own history and made sure that all the other routes now under Messenian control were blocked, reinforced and fortified against a Spartan attack.

Regaining Messenia became a Spartan obsession, for without the land which they felt was historically theirs, Sparta had neither the wealth nor the resources to influence the rest of Greece. Yet regaining Messenia would not be easy. The geography of the Peloponnese conspired to make even access to Messenia difficult. And to the exasperation of the Spartan leadership, by building Megalopolis, the Thebans and Arcadians had conspired to make it impossible.

The punishing lesson of the second Theban invasion was learned. The obstacle of Megalopolis was not going to be removed by brute force alone because the Spartans no longer possessed that brute force. Therefore diplomacy would be required. There were a number of cracks in the anti-Spartan alliance into which a diplomatic lever might be strategically wedged to prise the allies apart.

For one thing, by this time Athens was an active and vocal ally of Sparta, not out of any love for the Spartans but out of sheer terror at how mighty Thebes had become. The Arcadians themselves were engaged in a territorial spat with Elis to the north-west, for Elis claimed that in forming their League the Arcadians had incorporated several cities which they felt belonged to them. Spartan diplomacy worked at widening the gap between the Eleans and Arcadians – a long-term project that was eventually to bear fruit. The Arcadians did not help their cause by becoming obstreperous towards their Theban patrons, whom one Arcadian leader accused of being 'Spartans in all but name'. (It says much about how far Sparta's stock had fallen since the Persian Wars that what would once have been regarded as a high compliment should now be uttered as an insult.)

In 368 BC the Arcadians presumed too far on Spartan weakness when they began raiding Laconia on their own account. This provoked a retaliatory raid by the Spartans under the command of Archidamos, the enterprising son of the elderly Agesilaus. The Spartans in the punitive expedition consisted of new recruits too young to have fought at Leuctra and veterans of that battle who were desperately keen to expunge the shame of their defeat. Low Spartan numbers were boosted by mercenaries, Syracusan light troops and cavalry. When the Syracusans got into difficulties with a combined force of Arcadians and Argives, the Spartans came up in support.

It was well known that while other troops marched into battle to the sound of rousing martial music, the Spartans tramped in slowly to the sound of flutes. While other nations needed the music to spur them into battle fury, the Spartans needed music to cool their ardour. Therefore, with the Spartan phalanx still unformed, the Arcadians reckoned they had time to put their own lines in order before taking on the enemy. In this they reckoned without the depth of passion on the Spartan side. As soon as they found the enemy within striking distance the Spartans thought of nothing but attack. They dropped their spears into battle position and staged an apparently spontaneous come-as-you-are charge into the still unformed Argive and Arcadian ranks. (Despite this, Xenophon still finds time for an impromptu pre-battle speech by Archidamos in his text.)

Even with Sparta in its reduced state there was nothing like having berserk Spartan hoplites in their midst to create chaos and panic among the troops in a Greek battle-line. In fact, that line never formed properly as those in the process of forming up now dropped their shields and ran. This proved to be a grave error (in the most literal sense) because it exposed the disordered and fleeing troops to the completely fresh Syracusan light troops and cavalry. These turned what should have been a battleground into a killing field, as the cavalry rode down the broken enemy and herded them towards the spears of the pursuing skirmishers. According to Diodorus Siculus, 10,000 Arcadians and Argives were slain. While we have to allow for Diodorus' predilection for large, round numbers, it also has to be considered that if ever conditions were ideal for wiping out an army in the field this situation was it.

The Spartans, by contrast, lost not a man. Subsequently seen from the perspective of the winners, this was named the Tearless Battle. Yet as Plutarch remarks, this victory was less a return to warfare as normal among the Spartans than an indication of how much had changed. In previous years a messenger announcing a Spartan victory might be sent a cut of beef from the public mess in recognition of his efforts in bringing the news. Meanwhile life in the rest of Sparta would go on with barely any acknowledgement of the information:

> But when Archidamos returned on the heels of the tidings of his Arcadian triumph, nobody could hold back. First, weeping tears of joy,

his father came to greet him and then the Ephors. Soon a crowd of elderly men and the city's womenfolk were thronging the road to the river with upraised hands calling thanks for the blessing of the Gods. It was as if Sparta had erased her disgrace and things looked as bright as they had once before. They say that before this things were so dark that men were ashamed to look their wives in the eye, out of shame at their disgrace. (Plutarch, *Agesilaus*, 33)

In fact, the Spartan victory was not merely hollow, in that the only long-term effect was that the Arcadians made sure that Megalopolis was even more strongly fortified than it would otherwise have been, it was also counter-productive. Agesilaus was encouraged to believe that the courage of the Spartan hoplites would be sufficient to power the city through the current crisis and back to a position of dominance in Greece.

In the short term the major effect of the Tearless Battle was to drive Arcadia back into the hands of Thebes. Epaminondas led a further military expedition into the Peloponnese more as a demonstration of Theban power than with the intent of doing any serious fighting, but this was enough to impress the Arcadians into signing an alliance with Thebes. The fact that the Arcadians had gone from being Spartan puppets in the Peloponnesian League to being Theban puppets in a Boeotian Alliance did not pass unnoticed among the Arcadian cities. Mantinea was especially piqued, since that re-formed city had once been the greatest in Arcadia but was now secondary to Megalopolis and had become a Theban vassal to boot. The kaleidoscope of Greek politics shifted again as Spartan diplomats sensed that their former enemy Mantinea might yet come to be an ally as the Athenians already were and the Eleans were contemplating becoming.

Before this embryonic alliance could be nursed to full strength, Sparta had to face another potential disaster: the looming threat of peace. Corinth was eager for this, since Argos was again hostile, powerful Thebes was next door, and the Arcadian League was a worrying newcomer. Corinth's nearest ally, Sparta, was enfeebled and cut off. Athens was an ally, but so vulnerable was Corinth that Athenian interest was predatory rather than benevolent. Only advance intelligence prevented an outright Athenian take-over of Corinth, and realization of the city's exposed position forced the council to make diplomatic overtures to Thebes.

Decision at Mantinea, 362 BC

By now everyone was tired of war and a general peace was agreed. The one dissenter was Sparta. If they agreed to the peace, the Spartans would also be agreeing to the independence of Messenia, and this they simply could not bring themselves to do. Agesilaus still clung to the hope that his city's fortunes could be restored by war. As ever when a Greek city thought it was losing ground, the Spartans turned to the Persian empire – that great equalizer. It was the Spartan hope that the Persians, seeing the Thebans were a rising power in Greece, might aid Sparta in restoring the balance of power. The Thebans were aware of the danger, and sent Pelopidas himself to the Persians as their ambassador.

What had once been a matter of grave embarrassment to Thebes – that the city had never actually fought the Persians, and had even fought on the Persian side during the Persian invasion of Greece a century before – was now proudly recounted to the Persian satrap of Asia Minor as a reason why Thebes rather than Sparta should be preferred as a Persian protégé. The Persian satrap gave everyone a sympathetic hearing, probably because he was himself contemplating rebelling against the Persian king and to do so would need the support of Greek hoplites. (Greek troops were generally considered superior to their Persian counterparts, which was why the Persians usually let their money do the fighting in Greece on their behalf.)

Because Greece had been enfeebled by continual warfare and the Persian satrap needed a strong ally, the Persians came down on the side of peace. Athens and Sparta were ordered to stand down from their warlike postures and Messenian independence was given Persian blessing. It was a bitter blow to the Spartans, but Agesilaus had some ideas about how peace might yet be prevented from breaking out.

Arcadia's differences with the Eleans had deteriorated into open warfare, and the Arcadian League had taken control of the site of the Olympic games. This proved the final straw for the Eleans who now allied with the Spartans. Thus encouraged, the city of Mantinea announced that it was also leaving the League and becoming an ally of Sparta. With Mantinea and Elis on his side, Agesilaus started to provoke hostilities with the Arcadians, confident that the Athenians would lend their support – as indeed they did, sending an army by sea to avoid interception by the Boeotians. So much then, for peace. Rather than through representations at the court of the Persian satrap, the Greeks would settle their differences on the battlefield.

Epaminondas led a Theban army south and Agesilaus prepared to meet him. Epaminondas was under some pressure to fight, because his term of command was due to expire and he knew from bitter experience that the Thebans would punish him for holding command of the army past his due date. It did not help that his partner at the helm, Pelopidas, was dead. On his return from Persia, Pelopidas had set off on an ill-advised adventure in northern Greece where he had perished. It had always been the more popular Pelopidas who provided political cover for Epaminondas against Theban political in-fighting. Without his support, Epaminondas needed a victory to secure his newly exposed political position. His initial advance south achieved little, although he had taken his army far enough into Laconia to skirmish with Agesilaus in the very outskirts of Sparta itself.

From this skirmish comes one interesting vignette. When the Thebans attacked, the son of Phoibidas (the man who had infamously taken the Cadmeia at Thebes) was preparing for a visit to the gymnasium. As the Thebans approached, the young man snatched up a sword and attacked the enemy wearing nothing but a ferocious expression and a thin layer of olive oil. Despite his lack of preparation the young man slew several Thebans and suffered not a scratch in return. Afterwards, the Spartan authorities rewarded him for his bravery, and then fined him for going into battle improperly dressed.

Epaminondas withdrew towards Tegea, with Agesilaus following close behind. As he came out of Laconia and almost within sight of the walls of Mantinea (where his advance guard was savaged by Athenian cavalry), Epaminondas stopped to offer battle. In many ways the coming battle would be a rematch. Agesilaus was determined to prove that he was no Cleombrotus, and to show the rest of Greece that Leuctra had been an anomaly, and Sparta still reigned supreme on the battlefield. The climactic battle was fought on 4 July. As it transpired, Agesilaus was not present. The slippery Epaminondas had threatened to take both Sparta and Mantinea by surprise attacks, and Agesilaus was busy making sure that the approaches to Sparta were secured before he linked up with the main Spartan army.

At first it seemed that Agesilaus would be able to rejoin the rest of the Spartan contingent before the battle began. This was because after several long hours of manoeuvre and counter-manoeuvre, Epaminondas gave the impression that his army was done for the day. His men grounded arms as though they were going to make camp, with the left flank of the army secured against a nearby mountainside. As the Spartan alliance let down their guard, the Thebans stealthily prepared to attack.

To the great consternation of the Spartan alliance, the Thebans suddenly advanced directly on the Spartan and Mantinean contingent on the right of the allied battle-line. Troops to the right of the advancing Theban phalanx turned left, marched towards the mountain, and then faced right, joining the phalanx from the rear as it advanced. In a matter of minutes the Thebans had the same deep phalanx which they had used with such success at Leuctra. Xenophon, who undoubtedly talked to eyewitnesses, describes the Theban phalanx as pushing forward like the ram of a trireme cutting through the water.

As at Leuctra, as the phalanx on the left advanced those remaining men on the Theban right were ordered to hang back and decline battle. In case the Athenians and Eleans opposite did manage anyway to come to grips with the right wing, Epaminondas had put his cavalry and peltasts on a hill to the right. This placement threatened the Athenians with encirclement should they advance too far against the Theban right, for it would allow the more mobile enemy troops to swarm around their flank. Other cavalry forces were held in readiness on the left where they could exploit any gap created by the deep Theban phalanx should it succeed in breaking through the enemy right.

Apart from one detail, the Theban battle-plan worked perfectly. As planned, the phalanx crashed through the surprised and still disorganized Spartan and Mantinean line and broke it. Theban cavalry poured through the gap, ready to rip into the fleeing men. The allied centre saw its peril and likewise broke, leaving only the Athenians, protected as they were by their cavalry, which now deployed to protect the flank exposed by the broken alliance centre.

The one detail that Epaminondas had not allowed for was that he himself might fall in the battle. When word spread through the ranks that their commander was mortally wounded, the entire Theban army was gripped by paralysis. The cavalry abandoned its pursuit, while some elements moved to take on the Athenians. These cavalry units lacked proper command, arrived in small groups and were cut down piecemeal by the Athenian cavalry. The great mass of the Theban phalanx simply stopped dead where Epaminondas had fallen. It later emerged that Epaminondas and his subordinate commanders had all died in that first successful push, and as a result the Theban army was left leaderless.

Aftermath

This second clash between the Thebans and the Spartans turned out to be a losing draw for both sides. Until the death of Epaminondas, the Thebans had the battle won. Thereafter their loss of momentum and confusion handed the advantage to the Athenians, who remained the only organized force on the battlefield and they inflicted serious casualties on the Thebans as they withdrew. In the end, while both sides claimed the victory, both sides sent envoys to arrange for the return of their dead – something usually done by the losers in a Greek battle.

Thebes had now lost both Pelopidas and Epaminondas. Until then the city's people probably had not realized how much they had depended on the pair. Without the skilled diplomacy of the one and the generalship of the other, the makeshift alliance that the Boeotians had formed with the Thessalians, Euboea and Phocis began to crumble. Before long Thebes and Phocis were at war.

Sparta had not lost Agesilaus, as he was not present at the battle. However, many Spartans were muttering that this was not exactly a blessing. It is certainly true that it was on his watch that Sparta had gone from the most powerful state in Greece to a despised outcast in the southern Peloponnese. It is also true that the king's preference for brute force as a tool in international relations had resulted in the fatal weakness of Sparta's lack of hoplites being exposed sooner rather than later. Nevertheless, the long-term result would have been the same even if Agesilaus had been a skilled diplomat who relied on Sparta's prestige and presumed power to succeed at the negotiating table. Eventually the underlying issue of Sparta's lack of manpower would have been exposed and Sparta would have started losing battles.

At Mantinea the Thebans proved that Leuctra was not a one-off success. The Spartans *were* beatable – even at Mantinea, where the Spartans were trying hard to put troops in the field, the Spartan contingent was only a small part of the overall allied army. Without the threat of Spartan military prowess to force them to do so, no sane Greek nation was going to allow the Spartans to regain control of Messenia and use that land's resources to become a genuine threat once more. The Spartans were caught in a sort of Catch-22. They needed control of Messenia to become a first-rate power, but to gain control of Messenia they needed to be a first-rate power.

Agesilaus could see only one way to resolve the conundrum, and that was by recruiting mercenaries from the thousands of unemployed soldiers whom decades of warfare had created from destroyed villages and devastated farms. The problem with this idea was that Sparta, which had always prided itself on being an agricultural nation with little use for money, had no cash with which to buy the troops it could no longer supply for itself. Therefore if Agesilaus needed mercenaries, he must perforce raise the money by becoming a mercenary himself. This is why the final years of his life saw the king of Sparta fighting in the employ of one Tachos, leader of the Egyptians in one of their regular uprisings against Persian rule. Then when another rebel leader offered better incentives, Agesilaus abandoned his employer and switched sides. Plutarch remarks scornfully:

> He claimed that what he did, he did for the good of his country. It is as well he could veil his unnatural actions in this way, for without that pretext the only word to describe his conduct is 'treachery'. The Spartan idea of honour puts the interests of Sparta above everything else, and they can neither understand nor be taught any idea of decency apart from that which advances the glory of Sparta. (Plutarch, *Agesilaus*, 37)

Agesilaus served his new master faithfully – in part because that man kept a careful eye on him and partly because (says Plutarch) he was ashamed to change sides yet again. With the campaign successfully concluded, and a substantial fortune loaded on to his ships, Agesilaus set out to Sparta where the government was already hiring mercenaries. Bad weather and the onset of winter delayed him, and Agesilaus died without reaching his homeland. He was eighty-four years old and had been king for forty-one years. Archidamos, the son of Agesilaus, followed his father's example by serving as a mercenary to raise money for the state. He died fighting in southern Italy.

As it turned out, their efforts were in vain for neither Sparta nor the rest of Greece could withstand the forces of a changing world. The proliferation of leagues and alliances in Greece was a sign that the day of the city-state had passed. The future belonged to nations, and in the first case that nation was Macedon.

Philip II and the Macedonian Conquest

For centuries Greek and other suppliants seeking the wisdom of Delphi had left rich treasures at the site of the Oracle. This came in handy for the people of nearby Phocis. They had fallen out with the Thebans, who accused them of cultivating land that should be left fallow as it was sacred to Apollo. This accusation was laid through Theban dominance of the Amphictyonic League, an ancient confederation of cities which oversaw religious matters in Greece.

At this remove of time it is impossible to tell whether the Theban charge was well-founded or was simply a device to bring the Phocians to heel. Thebes was certainly upset with the Phocians because they had refused to contribute troops to the Mantinea campaign, and this fine may have been a form of punishment. (Justified punishment or not, the Thebans were definitely throwing their weight around, for while they were at it they persuaded the Amphictyonic League to levy a fine on Sparta for having abused the rites of Demeter to seize the Theban Cadmeia a generation previously.)

Phocis was subjected to a large fine, which it refused to pay. (So did the Spartans, who contemptuously ignored the demand.) Instead the Phocians seized Delphi and its treasures and used the money stored there as surety for hiring that same huge army of unemployed soldiers whom the Spartans had intended to use as mercenaries. Thanks to their financial reserves, the Phocians were able to hold on to their mercenary army despite repeated defeats until Thebes was financially exhausted by the effort of keeping its armies in the field. At this point the war had lasted into the mid-350s. At this point a new player entered the scene: Philip of Macedon.

Until now, the new Macedonian king had concentrated on securing the mineral-rich territory of Thrace, which had involved kicking the Athenians out of the region. That accomplished, Philip turned his attention southwards – and that attention was far from benign. In the guise of loyally supporting the Amphictyonic League, Philip led his men against Phocis and thus gained a foothold in central Greece. His defeat of the Phocians allowed him to claim their votes in the Amphictyonic League – an important concession because it meant that Macedon was now acknowledged as a 'Greek' state.

Such was the wealth and power of the Macedonian king that even the Thebans were subdued, especially as their long war with Phocis had drained their treasury and manpower (not to mention another war against the Athenians which had spluttered away in the background). Once the Thebans had reluctantly accepted Macedonian dominance, this left Sparta as the lone hold-out against Philip's power in Greece. The Spartans alone remained obdurately obstinate. To them the Macedonian king sent this chilling warning: 'If I come against you, and if I defeat you in war, I will devastate your farms, slay your people and raze Sparta to the ground.' The Spartan reply was laconic: 'If'.

As it turned out, a decisive confrontation between Sparta and the Macedonians was delayed because the rest of Greece decided to make a collective bid to destroy Philip's influence once the Macedonian king ran into a military setback in northern Greece. Urged on by the orator Demosthenes, the Athenians concluded their long-running feud with the Thebans and allied with them against Macedon. Philip's response was brutal. In 338 BC he marched south with his army and crushed the combined armies of Thebes and Athens at Charonea. The famed Sacred Band was wiped out to a man (with every man dying in his position in the ranks) and central Greece was left firmly under Macedonian control.

Philip did not want the city-states of Greece as his subjects but as his allies. His plan was to unite all the states of Greece and lead them in a war to defeat the Persian empire. To this end he formed the League of Corinth (also known as the Hellenic League), which included almost every significant Greek state. The newly independent people of Messenia certainly counted as such, and they too became signatories to the League. That alone was reason enough for the Spartans to stay out. Even now, the Spartans refused to take any part in any league or treaty that did not recognize Spartan sovereignty over their former possession.

When Philip was assassinated in 336 BC, the Thebans hoped that they could emulate Sparta's independence. After the defeat of Thebes at Charonea, the Macedonians had stationed a garrison on the Theban Cadmeia. This was hugely resented as being strongly reminiscent of the Theban humiliation when Sparta had occupied the Cadmeia and made Thebes a puppet state. Consequently, the Thebans were eager to throw out this garrison. They became even more eager when they received news that Philip's successor, his son Alexander, had also died. Such was their haste that they did not wait to check the veracity of this story. (In fact, Alexander had been wounded while besieging the city of Pelium in Illyria but the injury was not serious.) Urged on by Athens, the Thebans announced their unilateral exit from the Hellenic League and laid siege to the Macedonians on the Cadmeia.

Alexander wanted Thebes on his side for the planned invasion of Persia and therefore his response to the Theban attack was relatively mild. He pointed out that he was very much alive, and said he would take no action against Thebes if the two main ringleaders of the rebellion were handed over to him. The Thebans refused, believing they could hold off Alexander's army. Instead, the rest of Greece watched as Alexander stormed the city, burned it to the ground and sold the surviving members of the population into slavery. It was a grim end to a city which had been master of Greece just thirty years previously – though Alexander was cheered on by those Boeotian cities such as Orchomenus towards which Thebes had in the past been equally merciless. While the Spartans too might have felt a certain satisfaction at the destruction of the city which had vanquished them, it was also a sobering reminder that Philip's earlier threat to raze Sparta had been very real. (Thebes was rebuilt in 315, but never really recovered.)

Thus Alexander went on to launch the conquest of Persia without Thebes or Sparta. While they could do nothing about Thebes, the Macedonians remained piqued by Sparta's non-participation. This was shown by the pointed inscription that Alexander included with some of the spoils of his early victories which he dedicated in the Parthenon of Athens: 'These [spoils] were taken from the barbarians of Asia by Alexander, son of Philip, and by all the Greeks – except the Spartans.'

Very much *not* the Spartans, in fact, as they were considering joining the other side. Sparta was now under the influence of Agis III, the grandson of Agesilaus. At the time that Alexander was winning his first epic victories against the Persians, Agis took ship to the Aegean to plot with Persian ambassadors about forming a Spartan–Persian alliance. While in the region Agis noted that Crete was poorly defended, and sent his brother to occupy as much of the island as he could. (The brother was successful, but this opportunistic Spartan occupation was short-lived due to events elsewhere. Nevertheless an enduring link was formed between these two Dorian nations which thereafter lasted as long as did Sparta itself.)

For once a Persian alliance with a Greek state could not produce the pots of gold which had resulted from previous collaborations. The Persian king was simply too hard-pressed by Alexander to have many resources to spare for a Spartan attack on the Macedonian rear, however promising that development might appear. A relatively small sum of cash, some 30 talents, was provided, which was enough for Agis to recruit several thousand mercenaries. These mercenaries had recently been employed by the Persians. Defeated by Alexander, and ostracized in the rest of Greece, the exiled mercenaries had nowhere else to go and were prepared to fight for Sparta for a pittance.

In 331 BC fighting duly broke out. The Macedonian regent Antipater was looking after Alexander's affairs in Greece and Macedon while the king was conquering the east. The Spartans chose to open hostilities when Antipater was distracted by a rebellion in Thrace and had only a weak army in central Greece. This army Agis defeated, claiming Sparta's first victory since the Tearless Battle, and in consequence gaining the allegiance of the Arcadians and Elis. The Athenians (wisely) decided that they were staying out of the Spartan alliance. Nevertheless, according to Diodorus Siculus (our main source for these events) the Spartan alliance mustered some 20,000 men with Agis at their head.

By Greek standards this was a massive army, but the superior resources of Macedon easily trumped it. When Antipater did come south he brought with him a force at least twice that size. It appears that even at this moment of crisis, the Spartans could not relinquish their obsession with Messenia. When Antipater caught up with him, Agis had led his army to Megalopolis, the gateway to Messenia. Whether the rest of the Greek alliance would have allowed Agis to use an army that had been raised to fight the Macedonians to reconquer Messenia instead will never be known. Before he could attack Megalopolis, Agis had to fight Antipater's massive veteran army and this proved too much to ask. Sheer weight of numbers on the Macedonian side broke the Spartan force, and Agis himself perished in the battle.

According to surviving accounts, Agis died very much as a Spartan king should. He ordered his men to save themselves by any possible means so as to be of later service to Sparta. Then he himself, although so badly wounded that he had to fight on his knees, attempted to hold back the enemy. So viciously did Agis fight that in the end the Macedonians refused to close with him and dispatched the wounded king with a javelin.

The Spartan side lost over 5,000 men in the battle. It is certain that not all of these were Spartans, because Sparta did not have anywhere near that many Spartiates in total. Nevertheless, this battle – known to history as the Battle of Megalopolis – accelerated the already precipitate downhill slide in the number of surviving Spartiates. It did not help that the Spartans ignored Agis' dying wish and disenfranchised the survivors of the battle for their disgrace in losing the fight and abandoning their king.

The successor to Agis was his brother Eudamidas, who aggressively pursued a policy of peace. If the price for that peace was that Sparta would become a passive member of the Hellenic League, so be it. Eudamidas duly signed up, even though this meant that officially at least Sparta and Messenia were now allies. This was also the first time in its history (although the evidence is not completely clear-cut) that Sparta joined an alliance that was not led by a Spartan. Even when the rest of Greece rose up against Macedon on the death of Alexander, Eudamidas remained resolutely neutral.

In part though, Sparta itself had been one of the causes of this rebellion. Recognizing that the mass of unemployed soldiery in Greece allowed disaffected states such as Sparta (when it had the inclination) to raise large mercenary armies, Alexander ordered Greek states to take back their exiles. This caused considerable resentment, partly because the exiles were a somewhat lawless group, but also because others had helped themselves to the land and property of the exiles and were reluctant to hand it back.

There were other exactions also, especially of corn, and there was yet another reason for alarm among the members of the Hellenic League.

This was that Alexander's conquests and settlements in the east had resulted in a crop of new cities being founded across Asia Minor, the Levant and points even further east. Ambitious Greeks found a new frontier of opportunity opening up. The farmlands of Lydia and Mesopotamia were far richer than those of Greece and there were also opportunities for bankers, merchants and craftsmen that were far superior to the career opportunities available at home on the mainland. For the next half-century mainland Greece was to experience a massive population outflow that left behind only the very rich and the very poor. Alexander naturally wanted his new cities to thrive and the flow of emigrants from Greece was welcomed and encouraged. The city-states of Greece felt very differently, and added this to their list of grievances against their Macedonian overlords. When Alexander died, they rebelled in a short-lived affair later known as the Lamian War of 323–322 BC.

The wisdom of keeping Sparta out of the rebellion was confirmed for Eudamidas when initial Athenian successes resulted in another Macedonian army of 20,000 men arriving from Asia Minor as reinforcements. The entire war took around eighteen months, and the eventual Athenian defeat led to the forcible dismantling of the Athenian democracy and its replacement by a Macedonian-led oligarchy. Sparta was the last remaining fully independent state in Greece, although its people had to face up to the bitter fact that this was mainly because they were not deemed worth the effort of conquering.

Chapter 11

The Failed Reformers

Becoming Ordinary

The history of Sparta between 322 and 265 BC reflects a rather average Greek state which took part in the military and political struggles that had been an everyday part of Greek life since time immemorial. None of these struggles had any lasting effect in terms of territorial gains or losses, and Sparta as a society appeared to be settling into the role of being a second-rank city with a glorious past. What follows is a brief excursion through the highlights and lowlights of the half-century after the Lamian War of 322 BC.

As we have seen, the Macedonian rulers of Greece left Sparta alone in its corner of the Peloponnese – a corner rich in defensive potential and soldiery and with little worth looting. In Sparta the wealthy continued to get wealthier and fewer as the resources of the state were channelled into the hands of a prosperous but diminishing elite. Many average Laconians (and the average Laconian was now a poor man) leveraged the reputation of their glorious past to hire themselves out as 'Spartan mercenaries' in the many wars which the successors of Alexander fought among themselves.

During those fifty years the Spartan state itself did little to enhance its reputation. When the successors of Alexander did pay the Spartans any attention it was seldom benevolent. In the early third century Demetrios, the son of one of Alexander's successors called Antigonus the One-eyed, attempted to conquer the Peloponnese. He was in the process of carving out a kingdom for himself after his father's Asian empire had collapsed. Sparta's would-be conqueror twice defeated the Spartans but events elsewhere in Greece drew his attention away before he could consolidate his victories. The Spartans opportunistically followed up Demetrios' withdrawal and encouraged the citizens of the newly rebuilt Thebes to rebel against his rule. Then, when Demetrios turned on his pursuers, the Spartans hurriedly abandoned Thebes to its fate and returned to the Peloponnese. (Fortunately for Thebes, Demetrios was a mild man and Thebes was spared a second destruction in the style of Alexander.) Equally ingloriously, the Spartans became involved in the continuing quarrel concerning Phocian use of sacred land around Delphi. Having arrived there to enforce order, the Spartans got carried away with looting and were eventually chased off by the Aetolians.

One of the distractions that had prevented Demetrios from conquering Sparta was Pyrrhus of Epirus, that same king who had earlier fought and won battles against the Romans at such expense that his 'Pyrrhic victories' became proverbial. Pyrrhus was offered the chance to conquer Sparta by a candidate for the Agaid kingship whom the Ephors had spurned in favour of his nephew Areus I. The ever-opportunistic Pyrrhus jumped at the chance of gaining territory, especially since at the time King Areus and the army were away fighting in Crete (employed by the city of Gortyn in an otherwise irrelevant war).

Sparta still lacked walls, and as it presently also lacked an army this made the defence of the city very difficult. It was proposed that the women be evacuated, but Arachidamia, the elderly widow of the late King Eudamidas, bitterly opposed the measure. Thereafter Sparta's women took an active part in the siege of their city, personally building some of the entrenchments and acting as battlefield medics during the fighting. The defence of the city was ably commanded by Acrotatus, the son of Areus. Though no friends of the Spartans, the Macedonians liked Pyrrhus even less, and they dispatched reinforcements which enabled the city to hold out until Areus and his army arrived post-haste from Crete.

Despite Macedonian assistance on this occasion, Sparta and the over-lords of Greece felt no more kindly towards each other. Once Pyrrhus had left the Peloponnese in search of further opportunities (near Argos, where he died), Areus began to conspire with Ptolemy of Egypt. Combined with Ptolomaic interference elsewhere, this resulted in an Egyptian-sponsored rebellion against Macedon known as the Chremonidean War of 267–261 BC. This war is named after the Athenian leader who led his city into that rebellion. The inevitable result was that the Macedonians brought a large army south and yet again crushed Greek aspirations to freedom. From the point of view of this history, the significant detail is that as an ally of Athens, Areus led his army against the Macedonians and on to a devastating defeat near Corinth where he died fighting.

During this time Sparta had been steadily moving away from the Lycurgan principles which had been the city's social and legal basis throughout the fifth and fourth centuries. As we have seen, it was the early abandonment of the Lycurgan principle that the state should hold land and give it to each Spartiate at birth which had led to Spartan land becoming concentrated into the hands of fewer than a hundred families by the third century (Plutarch, *Agis*, 3).

It appears that by this time the traditional *agoge*, the stringent – and according to critics unnecessarily brutal – system of rearing young warriors was largely honoured in the breach. After all, there were few enough Spartiate boys to (mis)treat in this way. Those there were came from the best families in the state, who saw no reason why their sons alone should be brutalized.

Another change was that the Spartans, famous for their disdain for money, had now started minting their own. Formerly the Spartans had used archaic iron spits or iron coins tempered with vinegar to make the metal useless for anything else. It took a cartload of this to buy anything of value, and unsurprisingly Spartan coinage was refused with contempt elsewhere in Greece. This was all well and good, and as the mythical Lycurgus had doubtless intended. However, by the time of Areus Sparta's armies were not filled with land-owning Spartiates. At a rough guess, if every contemporary Spartiate of military age assembled for battle the city might muster 500 men; this at a time when Macedonian armies tended to be around 25,000 strong, and the Macedonians had several such armies.

Therefore Sparta did not even have enough men to fight its petty wars in the Peloponnese (the son of Areus died in yet another futile attempt to take Megalopolis), and had to hire mercenaries to do its fighting. These mercenaries needed regular pay, and for years the Spartans had used the coinage of nearby Elis both to pay mercenaries and to meet the expenses of their own landed aristocracy. Now Areus decided to do away with the pretence that Sparta had no use for coinage when the reality was so obviously otherwise. The first Spartan coins were minted in his name and were strikingly similar to their Macedonian equivalents.

The adoption of coinage was yet another sign that Sparta was becoming a normal Greek city – and indeed, there was no reason why it should not have been. The extreme militarization of its society had been necessary when Sparta needed to keep control of the richer and more populous Messenia. The old rule of thumb had been that every Spartan warrior needed to be able to defeat seven to ten Messenian helots if the city were to survive. This had resulted in Spartan warriors being very good indeed, because they and their society had specialized in nothing else but warfare. But Messenia was gone, and with it the need for Sparta's pathologically militarized society.

The fact that the primary reason for the previous excesses of Spartan society no longer existed did not stop many for yearning for the 'good old days' when the state was run firmly along Lycurgan lines. However, these traditionalists were balanced by others who preferred imported silks and properly cooked dinners to the former Spartan tradition of black broth and freezing morning swims in the river Eurotas.

Sparta's exceptionalism was still greater than the city's conformity with third-century norms for a Greek city, but that exceptionalism was now less marked than it had been before. Sparta even produced a philosopher called Sosibios, who had an interest in history. There was a final indication that Sparta was moving in the direction of becoming a normal Greek city. At around the time of Areus, the Spartans finally acknowledged that they could no longer rely on their own hoplites to keep the city safe. Like every other Greek city of any size, Sparta was finally surrounded by a defensive wall. In fact, given the city's natural position on hills alongside the Eurotas, the addition of walls made the city highly defensible.

Another way in which Sparta was similar to other contemporary cities in mainland Greece was that the population consisted mostly of those too poor to afford the costs of emigrating to the new lands opened up by Alexander and his successors, and those too rich to want to do so. Inequality was a major social problem everywhere in Greece, but especially in a society which had in its days of greatness prided itself on being a society of *homoi* – 'equals' (helots excepted, obviously).

Therefore Sparta's leaders had an interlocked set of issues with which to grapple. The first and most immediate was that Sparta was not only nowhere close to being a leading city in the Greek world (these were now places such as Alexandria and Seleucia-on-the-Tigris), but also the decline of Sparta was continuing. The number of Spartiates had long since reached a critically low level, and now the rest of the population was becoming increasingly resentful of the power and wealth which had accumulated in the hands of the remaining families. In short, revolution was ever more probable. The only question was, who would lead that revolution – those who wanted to overthrow the Lycurgan system or those who wanted to fully restore it?

In either case the losers would be the current Spartan aristocracy (for such the Spartiates had become). Like any group that holds power without adequate justification, this group was all the more determined to hold on to it no matter what the long-term cost to the state. 'These men shuddered at the name of Lycurgus like runaway slaves hearing the name of their master,' remarks Plutarch sardonically. However, also like all such groups, the aristocrats did not form a united bloc. Some were inspired by personal enmity of rivals within the faction and others were idealists.

Agis IV

Among the idealists we can certainly include the young Eurypontid king who came to the throne in 245 BC on the death of his father Eudamidas II. Agis IV was certainly a beneficiary of the current system, since his family was perhaps the richest in Sparta. Nevertheless, Agis was an admirer of the simpler days of old and on becoming king he immediately adopted those ways:

> He dispensed with all extravagances, put aside his expensive clothing and ornaments, and exchanged these for a short [traditional] Spartan cloak. He carefully followed all the ancient Spartan traditions in his meals, baths and general lifestyle. He plainly stated that if he could not use his power as king to restore Sparta's ancient laws and discipline, then he did not want to be king at all. (Plutarch, *Agis IV*, 4)

As is often the case with monarchy, the choices of a popular young king started a fashion among the rest of the youthful aristocracy. Suddenly young Spartiates were eagerly exposing their bodies to the rigours of a classical education, and looking forward to a future that matched the city's glorious past. In our sceptical modern era it is sometimes assumed that Agis acted at least partly out of a desire for personal power. Although king, he had come to that title at the age of twenty – too young to have developed that nexus of political friendships, owed favours and personal connections that would give a more experienced monarch his power. Agis would have found that more established characters stood in the way of his personal ambitions.

These characters included the Ephors, for the Ephorate had long been in thrall to the aristocracy who used bribery and personal influence to ensure that five of their own were elected each year. Another obstacle was Agis' Agaid co-monarch, a character called Leonidas II. King for a decade longer than Agis, Leonidas had the personal connections and social power base that the young king lacked on his accession. Therefore it can be argued that by starting his 'Lycurgan reforms' Agis was staging, if not a grab for power, at least a coup against those currently holding the reins of power in Sparta.

While acknowledging that Agis was indeed seeking supremacy in Sparta, we have to ask whether the modern sceptics are putting the cart before the horse. Did Agis use the power of the name of Lycurgus to become dominant in the state, or was his dominance of the state achieved out of a genuine desire to restore the Lycurgan constitution? This is a reasonable question, since if his channelling of dissatisfaction with the current situation was done purely to put himself in power, we have to ask what else he would want that power for. It would not bring more wealth as he was probably already the richest man in Sparta. It would not win him more respect, because he was already king. Therefore we have to accept that either Agis wanted power for its own sake, or he genuinely felt an obligation as Sparta's ruler to restore his city's fortunes.

Furthermore, if Agis had a personal motive, it was an entirely creditable one. Anyone who managed to restore Sparta to the position it had once held would gain not only power but also glory. Among the Greeks, striving for glory was not only an acceptable motive, it was practically obligatory for anyone who felt he had a realistic chance of attaining it. In fact, Plutarch explicitly says that glory was Agis' aim (*Agis IV*, 7.2).

Restoring Sparta's place in the world involved a great deal more than persuading impressionable young aristocrats to adopt simpler clothing and eat unpalatable meals. Agis saw clearly that wholesale reform of the state was required. He also knew there would be wholesale opposition to such reform, and he therefore needed both to find allies and to remove potential enemies. Stage one was to gain control of the Ephorate, which Agis did by getting one of his own elected to lead that group. This was a man called Lysander, who was a descendant of the famous Spartan general of the same name and was thus naturally interested in regaining for his city the prestige that his illustrious ancestor had won for it.

Stage two involved replacing Agis' co-monarch Leonidas II with someone more amenable. Leonidas had spent his youth in the east and was accustomed to the style of living suitable for an eastern Greek monarch. He had also found a wife while abroad. This lady may have been of Persian or Seleucid stock or even an admixture of both, but whatever she was, she was certainly not Spartan. If Agis made even reasonable headway with his reforms, not only would Leonidas' pleasant lifestyle be severely and adversely impacted, but his 'half-breed' sons would not be eligible for the succession. In other words, Leonidas could be expected to oppose Agis with all the considerable power at his command. Therefore at some point he would have to go.

For now, Agis continued to gather allies. Among those he needed most were his mother, with her immense wealth, family connections and debtors, and his grandmother, the now ancient Arachidamia who had all of the above advantages, plus the glory and fame of having led the Spartan women in their heroic repulse of Pyrrhus three decades previously. In his attempts to enrol the women of his family into the great reform project,

Agis found an unexpected ally. This was the king's uncle, a man called Agesilaus. Unlike his famous predecessor, this Agesilaus was more than somewhat avaricious and fond of the good things in life. Like his famous predecessor, Agesilaus was to prove ruinous to Sparta's fortunes, though unlike the earlier Agesilaus, the uncle of Agis was well aware of the damage he was doing.

The reason why Agesilaus was prepared to support Agis in his reform project was because he – like many of his fellow aristocrats – was deeply in debt. The basic problem was that most Spartan aristocrats were living beyond their means. The amount of wealth in Sparta was insufficient to support what Greeks in the wider Greek world now regarded as the basics of an aristocratic lifestyle, and Agesilaus and his contemporaries had been borrowing to make up the shortfall. Therefore, despite enjoying their luxuries, horses and slaves, many Spartiates actually owed the lot to their creditors. This was of little interest to Agis, though he was well aware that lower-ranking Lacedaemonians were suffering too. In fact, many of these struggled all their lives to pay off ruinous amounts of debt incurred from farming the marginal land which was all that remained to them.

If Sparta were to be set on a sound footing, this would have to include putting the state on a financially sound footing, so Agis proposed a cancellation of debts. This alone was enough to earn him the enthusiastic support of his uncle Agesilaus and the many other Spartans of all classes who were in the same straits.

The battle lines were becoming clear. On the one side were Agis and his family, his ally Lysander, enthusiastic youthful supporters and the mass of the people of Laconia. Added to these were aristocrats such as Agesilaus who were eager to be relieved of their debts. On the other side were those Spartiates who were doing very well out of matters as they stood, especially those more fiscally prudent individuals who were creditors rather than debtors. Being owed money gave the creditor considerable influence over the debtor, so these men stood to lose not only money but also political power. This group was far less numerous than the factions aligned with Agis, but it was the group that had held power in Sparta until the young king's accession to the throne. These men were not going to relinquish their hold without a fight, and they had a natural champion in the Agaid king, Leonidas II.

To tip the scales further against this faction, Agis also recruited the gods before presenting his proposals to the assembly of the Spartan people. (Such a proposal was called a 'rhetra'. It was a vestige of the democracy which had, in the archaic era of 700–600 BC, briefly made Sparta the most socially advanced city in Greece.) Agis brought the gods into the picture by discovering some oracles by a prophetess allegedly inspired by Daphne, a nymph with the power of prophecy. The pronouncements of the prophetess basically endorsed Agis' manifesto and warned the Spartans to beware of avarice and to return to the equality ordained by the laws of Lycurgus.

Then Lysander brought forward a proposal that the lands immediately around Sparta should be partitioned into 4,500 plots, each of which should be held by a single Spartiate. Since there were far too few Spartiates, Lysander and Agis proposed that the numbers be made up from free members of the Lacedaemonian community who were physically and morally of an acceptable standard. These men would become Spartiates and adopt the Lycurgan lifestyle of communal dining and constant military drill, while leaving their lands to be cultivated by slaves or helots. (Sparta still had helots – only those helots living in Messenia had been freed.) Children would again be subject to the strict *agoge* system of upbringing which would see them living in groups and subject to relentless training and discipline.

The other lands in Laconia would also be divided into lots, some 15,000 in all, and these would be allocated to those *perioiki* (non-Spartan Lacedaemonians) who were capable of bearing arms for the state. If this division of land went ahead, then at a stroke Sparta would gain an army of some 20,000 men with a hard core of 4,500 Spartiates. The number of 20,000 was not arrived at by chance. Later historians have noted that this has tended to be the size of any field army assembled for campaigning in third-century Greece, and it probably reflects the maximum number of men that could be sustained for any length of time by supply trains and foraging. A larger army would probably starve if kept in the field for long. Furthermore, because the mountainous terrain in Greece tended to offer cramped battlegrounds, a larger army could not be effectively deployed for battle in most cases anyway.

In short then, the land reform proposal Lysander put to the assembly offered the Spartans the chance to develop an army equal to any other that could operate in southern or central Greece. With such an army, the Arcadians might be cowed, Megalopolis captured, and Messenia reconquered. It was a giddy prospect. To take the first practical steps towards realizing that dream, Agis came forward after Lysander had made his proposal and announced that he and his family would start the ball rolling by contributing to the cause the lands of the young king's own very substantial estate, and the even larger properties of his mother and grand-mother. Furthermore, from his own pocket Agis would add 600 talents (worth very roughly fifteen million United States dollars today, though money goes a lot further when one has to meet only the basic require-ments of the average Lacedaemonian).

Leonidas predictably interposed an objection. He argued that Lycur-gan law ordered Sparta to expel foreigners. Yet here was Agis proposing that they should be allowed, even welcomed, into the ranks of Spartiates. Agis had expected the objection and had a counter-argument prepared. He replied that Lycurgus had objected to foreigners because of the vice, luxury and greed they would bring to Sparta. Since the state was already corrupted by vice, luxury and greed, adding foreigners was not – at worst – going to change much. At best, given that these foreigners would become Spartans and adopt Spartan ways, Sparta would purify the foreigners rather than the foreigners further corrupt the Spartans – if that were even pos-sible. In a final retort, Agis asked how the man raised in a foreign court, and with children by an oriental wife, could dictate that foreigners could not become Spartans?

Leonidas, backed by those who stood to lose their lands and the debts they were owed, forced through a measure that the proposed *rhetra* should be put to the *Gerousia* – the Spartan council of elders. The question for the *Gerousia* was whether the Laws of Lycurgus permitted non-Spartans to become Spartiates. If the Laws did not permit such an innovation, Lysander's proposal was not one that could legitimately be put to the assembly. It helped the cause of the reactionaries that one of the Laws of Lycurgus rather conveniently ordered that the Laws of Lycurgus should not be written down. Therefore the allegedly immutable Laws had a tendency to be whatever those currently in power wanted them to be.

Naturally enough, the wealthy landowners had over the years packed the *Gerousia* with their own, just as they had captured the other organs of government. Even so, it was only by a single vote that the *Gerousia* ruled – as was its right – that the *rhetra* of Lysander was not one which could be presented to the people. Therefore the measure failed because although the assembly wanted the proposal put before it, the *rhetra* could not be presented for the people to vote into law.

Leonidas' opposition had been key to the failure of the proposal. Therefore it was at this point that the reformers decided that the long-mooted deposition of Leonidas had to go ahead. The plan had already been laid and now Lysander put it into motion. This was quite trans-parently punishment of Leonidas for his opposition to reform – and it was intended to be transparent. The reformers wanted to show that they could be brutal if need be. This was to be less a legal challenge than a politically motivated lynching.

The charge was that Leonidas had taken a foreign wife, and Lysander demanded the death penalty for what Leonidas himself had recently argued was a violation of the Laws of Lycurgus. Leonidas correctly divined that since the *rhetra* of Lysander had now failed, those who had previously backed him no longer needed his support. His former allies would leave Leonidas to fend for himself. He had literally outlived his usefulness.

Two things prevented the Spartan king's untimely demise. The first was that the objective of the reformers was to take Leonidas' royal power rather than to take his life. The second was that his popular daughter Chilonis took her father's side and joined him when he sought sanctuary in a temple of Athena. (Later she followed her father into exile.) Leonidas was stripped of his crown, which was presented to his much more amenable son-in-law Cleombrotus.

Even with Leonidas out of the way, further obstacles remained. The reformers needed to find a way of redrawing their proposed legislation in such a way that it circumvented the ruling of the *Gerousia*. They were still working on this when Lysander's year in office ended. The new Ephors came as an unpleasant surprise to Agis and the reformers, for they were hard-line supporters of the reactionary faction. In fact, one of the first measures of the new Ephorate was to propose legal sanctions against Lysander for his actions while in office.

Still, the reformers now had both kings on their side. Therefore they argued it was not the place of the Ephors to oppose the united will of both kings – although some Spartans might have claimed with justification that this was exactly the purpose of the Ephorate. Although his stalled legislation was causing popular support to ebb away, Agis still enjoyed enough backing from the people to be able to take direct action. Followed by a crowd of supporters, he marched into the market where the Ephors met (at least some of the meetings of the Ephorate were public sessions). There and then Agis literally deposed the Ephors from their seats and replaced them with others, including his uncle Agesilaus. It was a coup in all but name.

Agis himself was a gentle revolutionary. He freed some prisoners, but left members of the opposing faction unharmed. Despite this, Leonidas was not prepared to take the risk of remaining in Sparta. He chose this moment to make a break from his sanctuary for exile in Tegea, and Agis not only let him go but provided his former colleague with an escort. This escort was needed because Agesilaus was all in favour of having the ex-king and his daughter meet with a fatal accident on their journey.

At this point Agis made a fatal error. He allowed himself to be persuaded by Agesilaus that even though the land reforms were currently blocked, there was nothing to stop debt relief from going ahead. This would at least show their supporters that the reformers were not totally ineffectual. Action of some sort needed to be taken all the more urgently because the Spartan army had been asked to aid their Archaean allies, and Agis would soon be away on campaign and unable to effect Spartan legislation.

The problem with separating debt reform from land reform was that nothing could have been better calculated to also separate the reformers from their political support among the landed aristocracy. Once their debts were cleared the aristocrats had absolutely no interest in giving up their lands. With Agis forced to leave Sparta on campaign in Arcadia, Agesilaus was left in charge of the reform process and made sure that the land resettlement became hopelessly bogged down in the legislative process.

With Agis away, Agesilaus settled down to full-scale abuse of his office. (Allegedly) he happily took bribes for unjust court decisions and even inserted a thirteenth month into the calendar so that he could squeeze an extra month's taxes out of the population. Unsurprisingly, the common people came to feel that the so-called 'reforms' had been a huge deception. Agis had used their hopes as the instrument to replace one set of corrupt rulers with others even more corrupt and with less constitutional authority.

Agis came home from his campaigning (where the Spartan army had impressed with its willingness, but there had been no serious fighting) and was met with huge popular unrest, which his enemies saw as an opportunity. The reactionary faction decided that before the newly returned Agis could get a grip on the situation in Sparta, they should risk all and bring Leonidas back from exile. Thanks to disgust with the slow progress of reform and the extreme unpopularity of Agesilaus, the counter-revolution succeeded. Restored to the Spartan kingship, a vengeful Leonidas now turned on those who had dethroned him in the first place. Agesilaus fled into exile and Agis was forced to seek sanctuary in a temple, just as Leonidas had done. The life of King Cleombrotus was spared because Chilonis, Leonidas' daughter, argued as passionately for her husband's life as she had once defended her father's. Cleombrotus was spared execution but went into exile nevertheless.

Agis remained in the temple of Poseidon and his friends took turns to escort him to the river to bathe. It turned out that one of these friends had borrowed a number of priceless goblets and other tableware from Agis' mother, and was loath to return them. With Agis out of the way, he would not have to do so and so he accordingly betrayed his king to Leonidas.

Arrested and brought to trial before the Ephors, Agis was charged with subversion, treason and the illegal overthrow of the previous Ephors. No one really wanted the young king executed, not least because he still possessed a measure of popular support. Agis was urged to admit that everything had been done at Agesilaus' direction. The hope was to show the public that Agis was a gullible young man who had been deceived against his better judgement, and that he now repented of his former folly. But Agis was having none of it. He firmly and resolutely claimed that what had been done was done by his orders, and he planned to do it again if given the chance.

By now the mother and grandmother of the king had turned up outside. With them was a restive mob demanding that the king's guilt or innocence should be decided in a public trial before witnesses. The panicked Ephors decided that Agis should be executed immediately. Then, when his mother and grandmother demanded to see that their son was safe, the Ephors had the pair escorted into the room where the 'trial' had been held and the king executed. The Ephors did not even bother with a further trial. Both mother and grandmother were immediately killed beside the corpse of their child – Arachidamia's execution being a particularly unsavoury act, as the woman was now well into her nineties.

Sadly, these deaths reflected another way in which Sparta was becoming a typical Greek city. Elsewhere in Greece political infighting was the norm, but it was still a merciless and lethal business. Sparta, with its stable constitution and social harmony, had heretofore been spared such disruption. Until the social consensus broke down with Agis, all but two Spartan kings had died peacefully. Of those two, one was Cleombrotus who had perished in the battle of Leuctra, and the other was a king so far back in Sparta's legendary past that he might not have existed at all. Certainly in all the previous centuries Sparta had never executed a king. The precedent was now set for an era in which Spartan politics turned deadly for all concerned.

Cleomenes III

This then, claims Plutarch (with considerable exaggeration), was Sparta in the years after the death of Agis:

The people were dulled by idleness and pleasure. All that the king [Leonidas] wanted was to enjoy his wealth in luxury, and he let affairs of state take care of themselves. The public interest was neglected and every man sought personal gain for himself alone. Now that Agis was dead, it was dangerous even to speak of practice at arms, hardiness and self-discipline, let alone of equality. (Plutarch, *Cleomenes*, 2)

While it seemed that the reformers had been utterly crushed, one of their number remained close to the centre of power. This was Agiatis, the former wife of King Agis, who had been spared execution as she had been at home during the crisis, caring for her young son. Agiatis was the heir of the deceased king and presumably also of his mother and grandmother. If so, this made her the richest person in Sparta. Not prepared to let all that lovely land and money go to waste, Leonidas forced the grieving widow to marry his son Cleomenes. (Of the young son of Agis, we hear little more apart from a disputable remark much later by the geographer Pausanias, who claims that the boy king was killed by poison (Pausanias, 2.9.1).)

So matters stood in 235 BC when Leonidas died and his son Cleomenes came to power. It transpired that Cleomenes had been none too fond of his father, but he was very fond of the wife whom Leonidas had foisted upon him. Love for his wife had gradually come to include love for the aspirations which Agiatis had shared with her former husband Agis. Cleomenes, in short, had become a reformer, though circumstances demanded that he keep that fact to himself for a while longer.

As a Spartan monarch, Cleomenes was first and foremost a military king. And as soon as the new monarch came to the throne, Sparta needed its king to be with the army. The problem was the Achaean League. This had grown out of the remains of the Arcadian League, which had split into a largely independent pro-Spartan element and the Achaeans who had combined to dominate the north-east Peloponnese. Under Agis the Spartans had allied with the Achaeans, but after the death of Leonidas, Aratus, the opportunistic leader of the Achaeans, attempted to expand his league by harassing Sparta's allies in Arcadia. The Spartans needed to show that the transfer of power to a younger king had not made Sparta any less able to effectively defend its interests, and so Cleomenes immediately set out with his army in a demonstration of force.

The first objective was to secure a valuable strategic strongpoint called Belbina, which commanded the approaches to Megalopolis. At this point the Achaeans and Spartans were not officially at war. Nevertheless, given that Sparta's actions were definitely unfriendly, Aratus decided he would follow a precedent from Sparta's actions in the Peloponnesian and Messenian Wars and open hostilities by seizing an unprepared city. A forced march by night took him to Tegea, a city that commanded the approaches to the Eurotas valley and the Laconian heartland. Here Aratus found that the locals had also read their history and were deeply suspicious of his intentions. The men whom Aratus was trusting to betray the city to him backed away from the plot and the Achaeans were forced to return home empty-handed.

Aratus was followed home by a messenger from Cleomenes, who pointedly enquired about what Aratus had been doing. The Achaean leader replied that he had been redeploying his troops in response to the Spartan occupation of Belbina. 'Really?' responded Cleomenes. 'So while your men were marching in that direction, where were your torches and ladders marching?'

Even though Aratus had failed to capture his objective in a surprise attack, the attempt still served as a *de facto* declaration of war. Given Plutarch's earlier denunciation of Spartan lassitude under Leonidas, it seems odd that once hostilities opened the Achaeans were very reluctant to engage Sparta in battle. Aratus was widely derided after an occasion when his army of 20,000 men refused to fight the 5,000 whom Cleomenes drew up against him. Yet when the Achaean army did turn to fight the Spartans in Elis, the entire Achaean force was routed. This would suggest that despite the calumnies of Plutarch, the Spartans had still been doing their battle-drills after all. (Not that the Spartans were yet able to muster 5,000 Spartiates in their army: the majority of Cleomenes' men were probably mercenaries, as the backbone of Spartan armies had been for decades.)

Cleomenes followed up his victory by turning his attention to Megalopolis – as the Spartans tended to do when they felt things were going their way. In any case Megalopolis was a member of the Achaean League and therefore a legitimate target. Again things went the Spartan way, and although the Spartans did not capture the city, they did comprehensively defeat its army and its Achaean allies right under the city's walls.

Given the Spartan warrior ethos, military victory was a sure route to popular support and political power. Therefore Aratus had unwittingly conspired to aid the reformers' plans, for until Cleomenes had gained credibility by his successful generalship he was little more than a figurehead on the domestic political scene. The Ephorate had a firm lock on power and exercised it ruthlessly. When Cleomenes' co-monarch died (presumably this was the youthful son of the late Agis and Agiatis, whom

Pausanias claims was poisoned), the Ephors were reluctant to accept his replacement. This was a reforming relative who had fled to Messenia when Leonidas staged his counter-coup.

When this relative was invited by Cleomenes to return to Sparta and take up the vacant kingship, the Ephors seized the man and once again executed a king without so much as the benefit of a trial. This proved unwise, because Cleomenes was nowhere near as mild as Agis had been – and Cleomenes had a loyal army behind him. When he returned home with that army, Cleomenes followed the example set by the Ephors. Without bothering with the legalities, he simply ordered the killing of every Ephor he could get his hands on (one escaped and was promptly exiled). Cleomenes had been doing his research while on campaign and, once the Ephors had been removed, he published a list of eighty other citizens whom he had decided were enemies of the state. These men were ordered to follow the sole surviving Ephor into exile.

After that the long-delayed reforms of Agis were imposed in full. Admittedly they were imposed at sword-point, but Cleomenes had no intention of becoming a dictator. He had effectively staged a coup against his own government, but he rejected accusations that in his attempt to reinstate the laws of Lycurgus he had perversely violated the most basic of those same laws. It was true that a long-standing tradition of civic harmony had been broken, but Cleomenes pointed out that the Ephors and their backers had started it. He claimed that he was more in the position of a doctor who has to cause some discomfort in order to purge a patient of dangerous toxins. Once the Laws of Lycurgus were restored to their rightful place in the constitution and vice, luxury and corruption were purged from the state, civic peace would be restored.

Even those whom Cleomenes had exiled were allocated lands, just as were the other Spartiates both old and freshly created. Once things had settled down, Cleomenes intended both to re-establish the Ephorate and to restore the exiles to their newly allocated lands. Likewise, Cleomenes wanted to restore the traditional joint kingship. Circumstances had recently been difficult for the Agiad line, so there were no suitable candidates to be had. In the end, Sparta enjoyed the innovation of a joint Eurypontid kingship as Cleomenes made a king of his brother Eucleidas.

This was not his only innovation. Cleomenes had seen the effectiveness of the pikemen employed by the Macedonians, and now he equipped some of his own men with the long two-handed *sarissa* and trained them in the formation which the Macedonians had used to subdue the rest of Greece.

Then he promptly led that reformed army out on a test run against Megalopolis and devastated that city's lands. Wisely, the Megalopolitans did not oppose the Spartans who, for the first time in decades, were able to make a military incursion into Messenia. Then Cleomenes marched north to Elis and again defeated the Achaean League, forcing Aratus to temporarily step aside from the leadership.

Sparta's dynamic young king was not yet done. With Corinthian loyalty to their League suspect, the Achaeans pulled much of their garrison from Argos to reinforce their grip on Corinth. Cleomenes took advantage of this and an Argive religious festival to infiltrate his men into the city of Argos. Taken partly by surprise, and partly (says Plutarch) by the sheer charisma of Cleomenes, the Argives agreed to leave the Achaean League and become Spartan allies. The uncomfortable fact of Argos and a resurgent Sparta combined against them was enough to persuade the wavering Corinthians to invite Cleomenes to evict the Achaean garrison from their city also. For a moment it looked as though the Peloponnesian League would rise again. The very prospect was enough to cause grave alarm to many.

Indeed, the undoing of Cleomenes turned out to be his very success, combined with Sparta's previous record of misuse of power when in control of Greek affairs. Sparta as a minor power in the southern Peloponnese was one thing, a Sparta threatening to regain its earlier pre-eminence was something else again. The people of Greece knew what it was like to be under the repressive Spartan thumb and had no wish to be back there again. Also, now that Cleomenes looked as though he might become a real power in the Hellenistic world, the established powers began to give Sparta their serious and very unfriendly attention.

One of the basic reasons why the Achaean League had come into being was as a Greek bulwark against Macedonian dominance. Yet Aratus (back in power) now opened negotiations with the Macedonians with the intention of allying with them against Sparta. It says much about the legacy of earlier periods of Spartan primacy that even the prospect of Sparta's restoration meant that the Achaeans and their Greek allies were prepared to accept as an alternative collaboration with what most still considered a Macedonian army of occupation. (Not that there was not severe dissatisfaction with the alliance with Macedon. Some historians believe that Aratus had opened these negotiations earlier, and it was partly this that caused the defection of Argos and Corinth to the Spartan side.)

In the new alliance some major concessions were made behind the scenes. The Achaeans agreed to restore the strategic Acropolis of Corinth to Macedonian control, and to give hostages – including the son of Aratus – for the League's good behaviour. In return, it seems that the Macedonians made a deal with Ptolemy of Egypt by which the Macedonians ceded to him some of their territory in Asia Minor.

This deal was necessary, because for decades Egyptian support was usually forthcoming for anyone who rocked the boat in Greece and made life uncomfortable for the Macedonians. This, in the Egyptian view, made it harder for the Macedonians to side effectively against them with the rival kingdom of the Seleucids. Also, the Ptolemies and the Macedonians were direct rivals for the possession of islands in the Aegean Sea. Consequently, Ptolemy had been funding the mercenaries in the Spartan army in the hope that this army would do as Aratus and others had done before and eventually challenge the Macedonians.

Instead, it appeared that Cleomenes had not fought the Macedonians – which was disappointing enough – but he had instead fought the anti-Macedonian Achaeans and driven them into alliance with Macedon. Furthermore, Ptolemy wanted Sparta as a regional trouble-maker not as a resurgent power. Therefore the proposal from the Macedonians was from the Ptolemaic point of view a win–win situation for Egypt. The Egyptians gained land in Asia Minor and made savings by dropping subsidies to their over-mighty Spartan ally.

From the Spartan viewpoint, being abandoned by Egypt was a disaster. Without mercenaries, the Spartan army was pathetically small, especially when measured against the combined strength of the Macedonians and the Achaeans. Cleomenes did what he could. First he raised some revenue by selling the remaining Spartan helots their freedom for whatever money those helots were able to raise. Then he vindictively turned on Megalopolis – the perpetual thorn in the Spartan side – and this time he did take and sack the city. This move came as a shock to the Achaeans, but the effect was not to split them from the Macedonian alliance, but rather to make that alliance closer.

In 222 BC a combined Macedonian and Achaean army advanced on Laconia, and Cleomenes had to march his outnumbered army north to defend Sparta. At first the Spartans were successful in holding the enemy back around Corinth, for Cleomenes showed himself to be an intelligent and aggressive general. However, once the Macedonians forced his defences at the isthmus a climactic battle for mastery of the Peloponnese could not long be delayed. The two sides met at Sellasia, on the northern boundary of Laconia. The result was an epic battle which caused severe casualties on both sides. The Spartans had high morale and a strong position which they held under a capable general. The opposing alliance had a veteran army, superior numbers, and very good commanders of its own.

Two key moments decided the battle. One was a cavalry charge by a young officer called Philopoemen of Megalopolis, which disordered the Spartan ranks. When the Macedonian commander asked who had authorized the charge, one of his officers replied that a youngster had done it without permission. 'Well, he showed the ability you should have shown, which makes him the general and you the youngster,' retorted the Macedonian leader.

The other key moment was a mistake by Cleomenes' brother Eucleidas. With the enemy advancing uphill towards him, Eucleidas waited until the last moment to counter-charge. He had wanted to tire the enemy with an uphill advance, but he left it too late. When the Macedonians withstood the first impact, they were able to push the Spartans back over the brow of the hill. This meant that instead of fighting a step-by-step retreat up the hillside with the slope in their favour, the Spartan troops faced superior numbers pushing them downhill. Packed together too tightly to manoeuvre and harassed by Illyrian irregulars, Eucleidas' men broke. Their downhill flight over broken ground cost them dearly.

Cleomenes meanwhile commanded the Spartiates in a toe-to-toe battle with the Macedonian phalanx. Though the Spartiates fought with a ferocity and stubbornness worthy of their ancestry, in the end the weight and experience of the Macedonians prevailed. Not many Spartiates fled, even after their defeat. Most died right there on the battlefield. Only when the Spartan cause was totally and irredeemably lost did Cleomenes leave the field.

Later the Spartans discovered that there had been a massive barbarian invasion of Macedonia. If Cleomenes had held off fighting for but a week or so more, the Macedonian army would have retired post-haste to defend its homeland. This it now did – but not before occupying Sparta. For the first time in its history the city of Sparta had fallen to a foreign invader. The revival under Cleomenes was over.

Chapter 12

Nabis and the End of Sparta

After all the bright hopes he had raised, Cleomenes came to an ignominious end. Following his defeat at Sellasia, the Spartan king paused only briefly in Sparta where he advised the civic leaders to make what terms they could with the Macedonians. Then he fled to seek sanctuary with his erstwhile ally, Ptolemy of Egypt. While Ptolemy was sympathetic to the royal refugee, he was not inclined to assist with Cleomenes' plans to gather a fresh army and return to Sparta. When Ptolemy died, his successor was even less sympathetic and Cleomenes was placed under house arrest. Eventually relations between the new monarch and the exile broke down to the point where in 219 BC, Cleomenes tried to raise a rebellion in Alexandria, and killed himself when that failed. His wife and children were then executed.

Meanwhile all was not well back in Sparta. The period between 219 and 206 shows the extreme state of dysfunction into which the city had fallen. For a start, Sparta lacked a proper government, for Cleomenes had slain the Ephors and had himself then been exiled and later slain. Of Eucleidas we hear nothing after Sellasia, and it is reasonable to follow other historians who make the assumption that he was slain in that battle.

According to Plutarch the Macedonian occupation of Sparta was brief since, as we have seen, the Macedonians had pressing business elsewhere. The Macedonians press-ganged the Spartans into joining a new Hellenic League (which never really got off the ground) and 'restored the ancestral constitution'. This latter is a claim by Plutarch, who does not really explain what he meant by it.

In reality it is very probable that with Cleomenes gone and the Macedonians decamped to the north, the old aristocracy attempted to restore its power. However, the reforms of Cleomenes had created a new class of Spartiates, and the survivors of Sellasia were determined that they should not have fought for nothing. This led to conflict as the old aristocracy attempted to reclaim its former power and the new Spartiates refused to give up their rights. The result was *stasis* – that dreaded condition of class warfare which had continually plagued other cities in Greece and wiped out the best and brightest of civic leaders while the others were engaged in futile, unproductive and vicious local politics.

Until 206 BC the record of events in Sparta is obscure and gloomy. Kings both Eurypontid and Agaid – mostly of questionable origins – were raised, exiled and recalled at a rate which meant that the average monarch lasted about eight months. Now that Cleomenes had set the precedent, at least ten Ephors were killed in civil unrest. The Spartan state had lost even more land after Sellasia thanks to Macedonian appropriations and Messenian opportunism, and the city looked as though it was sinking towards its own dissolution. At this point a final figure strides onto the stage.

Nabis Takes Power

Nabis was a villain, a black-hearted tyrant who revelled in torture and brutality. This is clear from the histories of Polybius and Livy, in rather the same way that if we are to believe Plutarch, Cleomenes was a sort of secular saint. There are numerous problems with our understanding of the reign of Nabis of Sparta. The main issue is that his history was written by the winners, as any history tends to be. Our main source, Polybius, was not neutral. As an Achaean he was attempting to persuade his Roman readers that the League was right to continue its feud with Sparta even after the death of Cleomenes. Any actions taken against Sparta were justified because Nabis was a very nasty person.

This bias is reflected in the work of the Roman historian Livy, partly because Livy at times follows the text of Polybius almost verbatim, and also because Roman conduct towards Sparta in this period was not particularly creditable either. Therefore an impartial reader is entitled to read accounts of the last years of Sparta as an independent state with even more than the usual scepticism afforded to ancient historians. Regrettably, our usual corrective, the work of Diodorus Siculus, is fragmentary at this point, though from the little he gives us of Nabis we see that he also was not a fan. For example:

> Nabis, the Spartan tyrant, continually came up with new torments for the people. He did this thinking that the lower he brought down his country, the higher he would raise himself in comparison. It is my opinion that when a scoundrel comes to power, he usually can't cope with his good fortune. (Diodorus Siculus, 27.1 (frag.))

It has to be admitted that if Nabis had been a gentler soul he would not have come to power at all. The struggle for the kingship was ferocious, and Nabis did not have a very strong claim. Polybius alleges – as he would

– that Nabis was only distantly related to the royal line. Nabis came to power as regent for the young Pelops when his predecessor in that position was defeated in battle by the Achaeans. Pelops was the son of a Eurypontid king called Lycurgus, whose own claim to the throne was so weak that Polybius claims he had to bribe the Ephors to accept it.

According to our sources, once he became regent Nabis promptly killed off young Pelops – and any other rivals to the throne he could lay his hands on – and set himself up as sole ruler. How much of this is true we simply cannot tell. We do know that members of the Agaid clan were rare even in the time of Cleomenes and times had been stressful since. The Agaids might have become extinct. It is undisputed that by 206 BC there was only one monarch in Sparta, and Nabis was definitely doing the ruling. Polybius assures us that Nabis held power through retainers who were 'murderers, burglars and bandits … the sort of men whose own countries had rejected them because of their crimes'.

Having come to power, Nabis appears to have been determined to avoid the fate of Agis, who had allowed his enemies to gather their strength in exile. Even abroad the enemies of Nabis were pursued, harassed, and not very discreetly murdered when the opportunity arose. For those who disagreed with him in Sparta itself, Nabis had constructed a sort of iron maiden: a metal figure designed to look like his wife, which was fitted with spikes that slowly impaled anyone pressed against it.

Either because he was too busy killing and terrorizing his fellow Spartiates or because he needed to rebuild the state after a disastrous war with the Achaeans, Nabis maintained a low profile in foreign affairs for the first years of his reign. Nonetheless, these affairs were getting interesting. Rome was in the process of defeating Hannibal's Carthage in the Second Punic War of 218–201 BC. In that war the Macedonians, led by the capable and energetic young Philip V, had taken the Carthaginian side. The Achaeans had stuck with their Macedonian allies, which naturally meant that the Spartans and Aetolians declared for Rome.

The Aetolians were another league which had arisen in the area just north of the Achaeans across the Gulf of Corinth. Though of long standing, the league had only recently come to prominence as rivals of the Achaean League. Unsurprisingly, the Achaean Polybius assures us that the Aetolians were a feckless bunch of opportunistic pirates, immoral and untrustworthy, whose bloodthirstiness was constrained only by their inherent cowardice.

Polybius does not tell us much about what Nabis was up to while he stayed out of foreign entanglements. The snippets he does give suggest that if the hostile tradition is stripped away, then Nabis was a reformer in the manner of Agis and Cleomenes but considerably more brutal about it. In fact, given that most of the opposition to his rule was going to come from the aristocracy, it was politically expedient for Nabis to take the reformist side. Thus we hear of him confiscating the lands of the aristocracy and distributing them to his raffish supporters. There are also tales of his selling slaves and helots their freedom. Plutarch mentions this act approvingly with Cleomenes, but Polybius describes it with the darkest suspicions in the case of Nabis.

In any case, after three years Nabis had overcome all organized opposition to his rule and had put together a handy army of 10,000 men. In the fifth or sixth century this would have been enough to strike fear into the hearts of nearby states, but times had changed. For a start, the average army in the Greece of Nabis' day was twice that size. Secondly, as Aristotle had cheerfully observed a century previously, 'When the Spartans were the only ones who did full-time practice at arms, they beat everyone. Now everyone practises and everyone beats the Spartans.'

Nabis at War

We hear that the first thing Nabis did with his army was to make a 'treacherous' attempt to gain Messenia. This was allegedly done by marching along a route which Polybius admits makes no sense whatsoever (Polybius, 16.13). Then, when beaten back by superior numbers Nabis somehow managed a retreat past Megalopolis as though that city did not exist – which it certainly did, having recovered, albeit imperfectly, from the depredations of Cleomenes. Indeed, Plutarch says that it was the army of Megalopolis which was mainly instrumental in ejecting Nabis from Messenia in the first place.

By this time Rome had finally defeated Hannibal, and now turned its attention to Hannibal's erstwhile ally, Philip V of Macedon. The Aetolians felt that the Romans had treated them badly as allies in the previous conflict so this time they allied with Philip. This brought the Achaeans in on the Roman side, and Nabis and the Spartans became Macedonian allies. Philip realized that the Spartans were loath to ally with the nation which had crushed their hopes at Sellasia. Therefore as an inducement he offered Sparta control of Argos, a city he had taken but had no hope of holding.

Nabis kept Argos under the control of the autocrat whom Philip had already put in place but sent his wife to raise revenue. According to Polybius, his wife was even nastier than her metallic image and in her money-raising efforts she 'surpassed even Nabis in cruelty'. This naturally left the Argives restless and resentful of their Spartan overlords. It did not help that those Argives who were too overt in their objections to the rule of Nabis had their lands confiscated and redistributed to freed Spartan helots.

It has been suggested by modern military historians that freed helots now made up the backbone of the Spartan army. It was definitely a realistic solution to a long-standing problem. In freeing and recruiting the helots Nabis no longer had the worry, common to generations of his predecessors, that the helots would rise in arms against him. They *were* in arms, but on his side. As a result Sparta no longer needed to keep soldiers in reserve to deal with the ever-present threat of a helot uprising. From the point of view of modern morality, the freeing of the helots corrected a major offence against basic human dignity. Ancient writers were less enthusiastic about such egalitarianism and penned indignant tales of helots marrying the wives of their former – now exiled – masters, with the assumption that Nabis must have compelled it.

Nabis had also renewed the long-standing association between Sparta and the Cretans. He converted the harbour of Gythium (the port of Laconia) into a full-scale naval base and allowed the Cretans use of this base to raid Achaean and Roman merchantmen. Doubtless many poorer Laconians took service as rowers in this rather *ad hoc* naval assemblage. In theory this raiding – decried by Nabis' detractors as piracy – should have stopped when Nabis realized the war was going against Philip V and adroitly switched sides. His price for betraying Philip for Rome was that he kept Argos and other minor territorial gains. Regrettably, the Cretans were slow to stop their very profitable depredations on Roman and Achaean shipping, and this attracted hostile Roman attention.

Consequently once the Romans had defeated Philip, they held an assembly of their Greek allies at Corinth. At this assembly the Roman commander Flamininus ordered the Spartans to relinquish Argos. The Spartans refused, arguing that a bit of piracy was insufficient to justify such demands. That the demand to return Argos was little more than a pretext for crushing Sparta became clear when the Romans left Argos in Spartan hands and advanced on the Peloponnese itself with 40,000 men. This was far more than a mere punitive force. It was evidently intended to be an army of conquest, especially when some 10,000 Achaeans were added to that number.

In the conflict that followed, the Spartans proved again that even if the composition of its army had changed radically, Laconia still produced some of the best and most stubborn warriors in Greece. Sparta was attacked, but held out – and holding out against a veteran Roman army was a feat that several of the greatest cities in the ancient world had recently failed to achieve. Even at the port of Gythium the vastly outnumbered Spartans fought Rome to a losing draw. They eventually surrendered the port but were allowed to march with their arms to join Nabis at Sparta.

At this point Flamininus was becoming somewhat disillusioned with the naked imperialism of his Achaean allies, and began to appreciate the value of Sparta as a counterweight to Achaean ambition. He offered terms which Nabis was prepared to accept, but which the Spartan assembly refused until a further round of siege assaults changed their minds. (Why the supposedly tyrannical Nabis put proposals to the Spartan assembly and deferred to their decision is something that Polybius does not explain.)

Argos revolted against the Spartans as soon as they heard that Sparta was under attack. It turned out that their rebellion was unnecessary, as the terms of the peace the Spartans eventually made with Rome was that Argos should be freed (whereupon it was promptly absorbed into the Achaean League). Also made independent were several other cities along the Laconian coastline that had been under Spartan domination for centuries. Peace broke out, and in accordance with his announcement that the cities of Greece were now 'free', Flamininus and his legions returned to Rome.

Nabis and his Spartans used their freedom to immediately start work on reclaiming the lands lost in the latest peace deal – starting with Gythium, without which Sparta was just another small, landlocked city in the southwestern Peloponnese. The idea of Sparta regaining even a shadow of its former strength greatly alarmed the Achaeans, who appealed to Rome. (Such appeals to the military power of the day were to become almost standard practice among the supposedly free states of the eastern Mediterranean – and not just by the Greeks.)

The End

The end of Sparta was sudden and brutal. Blocked by Achaean and Roman interventions into his attempts to restore Spartan power, Nabis reached an agreement with the Aetolians. The plan was allegedly that Aetolia and Sparta would appeal to the eastern kingdom of Seleucia for help, and between them crush the Achaean League while Rome struggled with the Seleucids. The plan was quashed by prompt Achaean and Roman intervention, whereupon the frustrated Aetolians killed Nabis and took Sparta.

In the story as we have it, the Aetolians had basically decided that they were not going to beat the Roman–Achaean alliance, and so decided to take Sparta as a sort of compensation prize. They had given Sparta reinforcements of 1,000 men to defend the city against an Achaean assault (an assault which Roman diplomats were vigorously attempting to prevent, which seems strange and inconsistent if Sparta were really conspiring with Rome's enemies).

While Nabis was watching the Aetolians at drill one of their number abruptly turned on him and killed him with his lance. The Aetolians then tried to gain control of Sparta as a whole, but were instead massacred to a man by the indignant Spartan people: that is, those same people whom Nabis was allegedly controlling through tyranny and terror. Thereupon the Achaeans stepped in to stop the turmoil in Sparta by taking the leaderless and demoralized city by an assault which was barely resisted.

There is much that is unsatisfactory here and parts of this narrative appear to defy logic. We can fairly accuse Polybius of dissembling, in that his description of what happened to Nabis is deeply suspect. The fact that these events led to the Achaeans taking over Sparta despite Roman objections makes the entire narrative appear somewhat disingenuous.

However, one fact remains indisputable. By whatever means and in whatever manner, Nabis was killed in 192 BC. With him ended not only the last chance for reform of the Spartan state but also the existence of Sparta itself as an independent entity. Sparta continued to exist for centuries to come, but never again was it more than a small Peloponnesian mountain town under the control of others.

Aftermath

The Achaeans were determined to make Sparta a 'normal' Hellenic city, albeit one totally under their power. The Spartan army was made little more than an honour-guard and the city walls were thrown down. The Lycurgan Laws were abolished and the aristocratic exiles encouraged to return and set up an oligarchy. Predictably, this did not quash the simmering social unrest in Sparta, and relationships with the Achaean League were tetchy at best. Eventually the Roman senate tired of the constant bickering between Sparta and the rest of the League and ordered that Sparta and several other League cities be allowed independence. It was in part the League's refusal to conform that caused the Roman intervention of 146 BC, and the absorption of Greece – including Sparta – into Rome's growing empire.

As a Roman city, the Spartans were allowed to return to their traditional ways. This was less to encourage a military tradition than because Roman tourists were keen to see the old Spartan lifestyle in action. Seats were set up so that visiting spectators could watch some of the more painful feats of endurance suffered by Spartan children as they went through the rites of the *agoge*. 'Because an oracle told them that they should stain the altar [of Artemis Orthia] with human blood ... Lycurgus made it traditional for the Spartans to have young men whipped there,' Pausanias tells his Roman readers (Pausanias, 3.16.10). The young men had to run a gauntlet to this altar and were so severely whipped in the process that some died. Paying spectators lined the walls of the enclosure for the show. In short, Roman Sparta became a sort of gruesome theme park mimicking the rituals of its glorious past.

Roman emperors were not above exploiting that past. At least two third-century emperors had a Spartan contingent in their armies, almost certainly for their propaganda value. When Rome fell, Sparta went down with the empire. The town was sacked by the barbarian war-leader Alaric in AD 396 and was abandoned before the Slavic occupation of the Peloponnese during the following centuries.

It is possible that a small population continued to live in the ruined city, but most locals were in the new fortified foundation of Mystras, which was the most important settlement in the area for most of the late Byzantine and Ottoman eras. The city of Sparta itself was re-established in the modern era and today Sparta is home to some 20,000 citizens. Many of these, like their predecessors of the Roman era, make a living from tourists visiting a site that was so influential in European history. Like the Romans, many tourists still visit the (now restored) temple of Artemis Orthia.

Laconophilia

Though fallen, Sparta has not lost its power to influence the modern world. The city is celebrated in film, computer games, novels and macho TV reality programmes. In fact, it would be fair to say that Sparta has more admirers in the modern world than ever it had in the city's heyday. The Spartan virtues seen most clearly at Thermopylae continue to inspire us today – comradeship in adversity, self-sacrifice and courage are universally celebrated values and remain worthy aspirations.

Less encouraging have been more literal attempts to emulate Sparta in the modern world, as generations of schoolboys brought up in the English public school system can attest. These schools were set up in the nineteenth century to raise the scions of the upper classes as colonial administrators. In conscious emulation of the Spartan *agoge* system (albeit stripped of its more horrific features) the schools raised their pupils in single-gender packs called 'houses' and celebrated character development through hardship. As the novelist Evelyn Waugh remarked, 'Anyone who has been to an English public school will always feel comparatively at home in prison.'

Even more malevolent was the influence of Sparta on Nazi philosophy. This has been shown in works such as *Sparta in Modern Thought* (Stephen Hodkinson and Ian MacGregor Morris (eds), Classical Press of Wales, 2010), and even more transparently in the writing of Adolf Hitler himself. In his *Mein Kampf* Hitler explicitly endorses the Spartan ideals of the supremacy of the state over the individual and the celebration of the warrior ethos. Unsurprisingly, the intellectual roots of National Socialism can be found in philosophers such as Nietzsche and Muller, who were ardent Hellenphiles and admirers of Sparta. Even today, a quick web search reveals 'manifestos' such as this:

Ancient Sparta and National Socialist Germany: two States – symbols of the struggle for the right and the truth, in the fight for the downfall of the social plague of democracy and bolshevism [sic]. Even though Berlin has fallen, even though the Medes passed through Thermopylae ... The New Thermopylae have not fallen yet, the New Thermopylae

will be Triumphant, the New Thermopylae are our Souls!
(https://phosphorussite.wordpress.com)

It would be easy, but incorrect to dismiss these as perversions of the Spartan ideal. However, a reading of the Laconophile Plato's *Republic* will show the same chilling disregard for the individual, and sentiments such as that children are the property of the state, and 'sub-standard' persons should be ruthlessly eliminated from the breeding stock. And Plato modelled his ideas on a state he knew personally.

Interestingly, the more than somewhat Laconophobic Aristotle attributes Sparta's fall to exactly those principles which Laconophiles admire today:

> Their whole system of laws is directed at developing only a single aspect of virtue – military valour, because this is necessary for conquest. This certainly kept the state secure while it was at war. However, it also threw the state into decline once it had won itself an empire, because the Spartans did not know how to relax. They had no training in those things that are more important than war. (Aristotle, *Politics*, 1271b)

Bibliography

Blockley, R.C., 'Dexippus and Priscus and the Thucydidean Account of the Siege of Plataea', *Phoenix*, 1972 (26): 18–27.

Cartledge, P., *Sparta and Lakonia: a regional history 1300–362 BC* (2013).

Figueira, T.J., 'Population Patterns in Late Archaic and Classical Sparta', *Transactions of the American Philological Association*, 1974 (116): 165–213.

Flower, M.A., 'Revolutionary agitation and social change in classical Sparta', *Bulletin of the Institute of Classical Studies*, 1991 (37): 78–97.

Forrest, W.G., *History of Sparta* (Bristol Classical Press, 1998).

Hodkinson, S., 'Land tenure and Inheritance in Classical Sparta', *Classical Quarterly*, 1986/2009 (36.2): 378–406.

Property and Wealth in Classical Sparta (Classical Press of Wales, 2009).

Hutchinson, G., *Sparta: Unfit for Empire* (Casemate, 2015).

Michalopoulos, M., *In the Name of Lykourgos: The Rise and Fall of the Spartan Revolutionary Movement (243–146BC)* (Casemate, 2017).

Plant, I.M., 'The Battle of Tanagra: A Spartan Initiative?' *Historia*, 1994 (43): 259–74.

Powell, A., *Classical Sparta: Techniques Behind Her Success* (Routledge Revivals, 2014).

Powell, A. and Hodkinson, S. (eds), *Sparta: The Body Politic* (Classical Press of Wales, 2010).

bibliography

Index